Sizing Up Measurement

Sizing Up Measurement

Activities for Grades K–2 Classrooms

Vicki Bachman

Math Solutions Publications
Sausalito, CA

Math Solutions Publications
A division of
Marilyn Burns Education Associates
150 Gate 5 Road, Suite 101
Sausalito, CA 94965
www.mathsolutions.com

Library of Congress Cataloging-in-Publication Data

Bachman, Vicki.
  Sizing up measurement. Activities for grades K–2 classrooms / Vicki Bachman.
    p. cm.
  Includes bibliographical references and index.
  ISBN-13: 978-0-941355-79-7
  ISBN-10: 0-941355-79-9
  1. Mensuration. 2. Mathematics—Study and teaching (Elementary)—Activity programs. [1. Measurement.] I. Title.
QA465.B127 2007
372.35'044—dc22
                                        2007018882

Editor: Toby Gordon
Production: Melissa L. Inglis
Cover design: Isaac Tobin
Interior design: Jenny Jensen Greenleaf
Composition: ICC Macmillan Inc.

Printed in the United States of America on acid-free paper
11 10 09 08 07 ML 1 2 3 4 5

To my family and friends,
with special thanks to Peter
for his extraordinary patience

A Message from Marilyn Burns

We at Math Solutions Professional Development believe that teaching math well calls for increasing our understanding of the math we teach, seeking deeper insights into how children learn mathematics, and refining our lessons to best promote students' learning.

Math Solutions Publications shares classroom-tested lessons and teaching expertise from our faculty of Math Solutions Inservice instructors as well as from other respected math educators. Our publications are part of the nationwide effort we've made since 1984 that now includes

- more than five hundred face-to-face inservice programs each year for teachers and administrators in districts across the country;
- annually publishing professional development books, now totaling more than sixty titles and spanning the teaching of all math topics in kindergarten through grade 8;
- four series of videotapes for teachers, plus a videotape for parents, that show math lessons taught in actual classrooms;
- on-site visits to schools to help refine teaching strategies and assess student learning; and
- free online support, including grade-level lessons, book reviews, inservice information, and district feedback, all in our quarterly *Math Solutions Online Newsletter*.

For information about all of the products and services we have available, please visit our website at *www.mathsolutions.com*. You can also contact us to discuss math professional development needs by calling (800) 868-9092 or by sending an email to *info@mathsolutions.com*.

We're always eager for your feedback and interested in learning about your particular needs. We look forward to hearing from you.

Math Solutions®
PUBLICATIONS

Contents

6 Temperature 122

Blackline Masters 131

Introduction

Measurement is one of the very earliest forms of mathematics. For centuries people have measured quantities to cook, to build, to make clothing, to divide land, and to keep track of time and distance. In recent years, our abilities to measure have expanded dramatically; we now measure in order to travel through space, to fabricate molecular-size devices, and to create global positioning systems.

Certainly children use measurement in their daily lives, too, as they compare heights, see how far they can run and jump, keep track of how many days until their birthdays, compare their ages, and celebrate each time they need the next shoe size. As children grow older, they may become interested in sports statistics or world records involving measurement; they may use measurement to rearrange furniture or their rooms or to build items such as birdhouses or model rockets. Clearly measurement must be an important part of the mathematics curriculum, as it helps students make mathematical sense of their lives and prepares them for their future.

Unfortunately, it is easy for teachers to become overwhelmed with the abundance of measurement objectives they are asked to address; teachers often resort to dealing with those objectives by telling students what to memorize. For students who experience this kind of incomplete instruction, measurement becomes a list of terms, numbers, and facts that they easily forget.

We too have encountered the complexities of teaching measurement in our classrooms. We know that it is very easy to become overwhelmed by all that is expected of us. But we also have experienced the joys of teaching measurement in ways that help our students make sense of the mathematics they are learning. We've seen our students come away from these lessons excited about their new and deeper understandings of measurement. We've watched our students develop confidence in their ability to use measurement to understand their world rather than struggle to simply memorize rote formulas. These are the kinds of lessons we want to share with you here.

In this three-book series, Sizing Up Measurement, we have worked to create lessons that focus on essential measurement concepts that are connected to problem-solving contexts. The lessons focus on helping students

◈ identify the attribute to be measured (for example, length or weight);

◈ know what it means to measure—comparing the attribute of the item or situation with a unit with the same attribute: lengths must be compared with units of length, areas with units of area, and so on;

◈ develop an understanding of what it means to measure using standard and non-standard units;

◈ select a system of measurement to be used—customary or metric;

◈ understand how benchmark units—such as *a centimeter is about the width of a pencil*—help determine the magnitude of specific units;

◈ estimate the result of the measurement, both before and after the act of measuring;

◈ select a measurement tool to assign a number value and determine how accurate they need to be; and

◈ keep track of results in an organized and useful way.

As you can imagine, given the grade-level spans in this series (K–2, 3–5, 6–8), the three books deal with very different levels of mathematics, but there are commonalities among them all. Each of the books includes lessons that relate to categories of measurement important for that grade-level span, and the lessons in all three books provide meaningful contexts for students to solve problems and use their mathematical skills as they develop important vocabulary related to measurement.

Before trying these lessons, it is important to consider the natural progressions in thinking that children pass through as they develop basic concepts of measurement:

When your student lays down toothpicks to measure length and leaves gaps or overlaps the toothpicks, the student is struggling with *unit iteration*. He doesn't yet understand that the distance of the units altogether should be equal to the distance being measured.

When your student thinks that, when measuring with small units, a small total should result, the student does not yet know the *inverse relationship* between the size of the unit and the number of units—small units create a larger total and large units create a smaller total.

When your student compares the length of pencils that are not evenly lined up and thinks that the pencil that sticks out is longer, the student has not yet developed *conservation of length*—the idea that a different position does not change the length.

When your student knows that the marker is shorter than the pencil, and the pencil is shorter than the stick, but doesn't realize the marker therefore must be shorter than the stick, the student has yet to develop *transitive reasoning*. This is necessary in order for children to understand how rulers help us compare objects that are not side by side.

When you put a pencil against the ruler between 2 and 8, and a student thinks the pencil is 8 inches long, the student doesn't understand that the number on the ruler represents the entire distance from the "zero end" to that number.

When a student thinks an angle with longer sides has a larger measure, the student doesn't understand that the measure of an angle depends upon the spread of the angle's rays.

When a student thinks it is impossible to determine the area of an irregular polygon, the student may not understand that figures can be partitioned into shapes that have areas that she can determine.

When a student assumes that a constant perimeter always yields a constant area, the student does not understand the relationship between these two measures.

When a student depends upon a separate formula for determining the volume of each kind of prism and pyramid, the student does not understand the relationships among the volumes of such figures.

The lessons in these books are intended to provide students with opportunities to make sense of these and other critical understandings related to measurement. Through multiple experiences with length, area, capacity and volume, mass and weight, temperature, and time, students learn how to measure, compare, and order. Measurement requires estimation, making comparisons, mental math, and number sense. Students need to add, subtract, multiply, divide, and perceive numerical relationships in many different ways. Measurement is a topic that deserves attention and time in every school year. We offer these lessons in the hopes that you will use and adapt them to fit your circumstances. All students need many opportunities to build their understandings, make connections to other topics, explain their thinking and procedures, and analyze and communicate their results to others. We sincerely hope that you and your students enjoy these lessons.

VICKI BACHMAN, GRADES K–2
CHRIS CONFER, GRADES 3–5
ANN LAWRENCE AND CHARLIE HENNESSY, GRADES 6–8

Length

Introduction

Before our students get to school they have a lot of experience with linear measurement. Their ability to reach things and to be independent is directly connected to length. They are very aware of their personal height in comparison with others and they are constantly growing out of everything from clothes to shoes to beds. Informal observations and comparisons of measurements of length are part of our students' everyday lives.

Kindergarten, first-, and second-grade students need many varied experiences and explicit instruction to bridge their informal understandings to the mathematical ideas and vocabulary of linear measurement. It is our job to build on what children know and are able to do and eventually introduce to them standard units of measure such as centimeters, inches, and feet.

The fifteen length lessons increase in complexity as the chapter progresses. Early lessons focus on making direct comparisons, whereas later lessons include concepts such as perimeter, doubling, and halving, often using standard units of measurement.

Many lessons involve some choice of measurement tool so that students can compare and discuss a variety of results. All of the lessons involve making predictions, solving problems, and communicating with others.

Rod Towers

Overview

In this lesson children build and then determine the height of Cuisenaire rod towers. Students build a tower with a partner, decide the measurement tool to use, measure their tower, and then in a whole-class discussion make comparisons between the towers.

Materials

◈ Cuisenaire rods and/or blocks, 1 shoebox-size tub per pair of students

◈ measuring tools such as string or yarn cut into lengths of about 3 feet, measuring tapes, connecting cubes, yardsticks, meter sticks, and 1-inch cubes, enough so that partners have a choice of measuring tools

Vocabulary: cities, compare, Cuisenaire rods, height, long, longer, longest, measure, scarce, short, shorter, shortest, skyscraper, small, smaller, smallest, space, tall, taller, tallest, tower, vertical

Instructions

1. Prior to this lesson, provide a session for the children to explore the Cuisenaire rods or blocks. Once children are comfortably acquainted with the materials, ask them to describe what they notice. Discuss the variations among the materials and focus on similarities and differences to develop mathematical vocabulary.

2. Begin *Rod Towers* by explaining that tall buildings in cities are called *skyscrapers*. Ask the children why that name might have become popular. Explain that tall buildings are found mostly in cities because people build upward when land is scarce. Ask the children to tell about tall buildings that they have seen. Ask them to describe some of the things that might be involved in constructing a tall building.

3. Explain to the students that they are going to work with a partner to build a tower and then measure its height. Show the children how to position the Cuisenaire rods: beginning with the two longest rods and placing them parallel to one another, then stacking the next two in the opposite direction, and continuing upward, eventually decreasing by size as they go. Discuss the kind of cooperation it will take to work together to build a tower. Have several children share ideas about fair teamwork. When the expectations have been established, describe the procedures for distributing available materials.

4. Organize the class into partners. Let the children know how much work time they will have by using a timer or by establishing a stopping point on a clock in the room. Explain that when it is time to stop building, you will give a signal, and each

pair will decide how to measure their tower. Show the children the variety of measurement tools that they may choose from.

5. After the children have had a reasonable amount of time (about fifteen minutes) to build, stop the class and ask students to find a way to describe how tall their buildings are. Some of the children may use their bodies to make a direct comparison by standing next to the tower, holding their hands up to the top of the tower, and saying, for instance, "It's up to my stomach!" Ask the children if they think that any of the towers are the same height and discuss ways that students might determine the answer without moving the towers.

6. Next, have partners decide on a measuring tool, measure their tower, and then, when everyone is ready, report back to the class about the height of their structure. Most likely, you will hear comments like "This is how far our tower comes up on the meter stick," "Our tower was twenty-six cubes tall," and "Our tower was thirty-one blocks high." Discuss the various measurement methods the children used.

7. Have children, either alone or in pairs, draw their tower and label it with its height. Save these illustrations so that the children can compare the heights from this lesson with those of towers they build in the future.

Extensions
◈ Have children build two towers of the same height out of different materials.
◈ Have children create a tower and then build another that is twice the height or half the height of the original.
◈ Challenge the children to build an inverted tower, with the smallest blocks on bottom.
◈ Have children create drawings of tall buildings and describe the relative heights.

 Yarn-Length Hunt

Overview
In this activity, children use pieces of yarn to develop concepts and vocabulary related to length comparisons. Students first compare their yarn pieces with one another; then they form a line that shows the order of the yarn lengths. Finally, each student finds two or three objects in the classroom that are longer than his or her piece of yarn and two or three objects in the room that are shorter.

Materials
◈ length-related books such as *How Tall, How Short, How Far Away*, by David Adler (1999) and *Carrie Measures Up!* by Linda Williams Aber (2001)

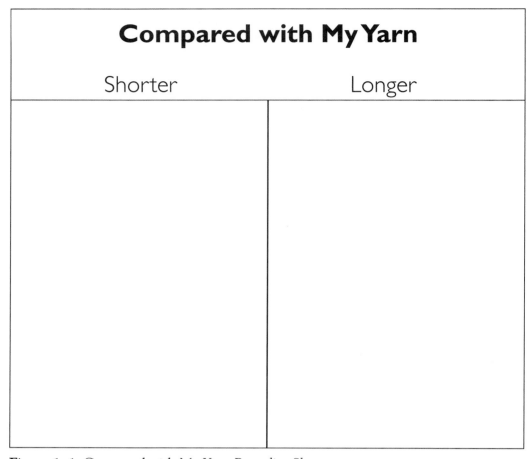

Compared with My Yarn

Shorter	Longer

Figure 1–1 Compared with My Yarn *Recording Sheet*

- ❧ yarn cut to 4 different lengths ranging from 5 inches to a foot, 1 per student (make an equal number of pieces for each yarn length)
- ❧ 3-by-5-inch index cards, 10 to 20
- ❧ optional: *Compared with My Yarn* recording sheets, 1 per student (see Figure 1–1; see also Blackline Masters)
- ❧ optional: a collection of objects to be measured

Vocabulary: beginning, compare, end, height, length, line, longer, longest, measure, order, same, shorter, shortest

Instructions

1. Before class, prepare some word cards for the lesson. Write the words *compare*, *measure*, and *length*, one on each of three index cards. If you don't have a math word wall, you might consider creating one.

2. Read a book that involves an attribute of length or height (see "Materials" list). Discuss the mathematical focus of the story.

3. Show the children one piece of the cut yarn and ask the class to describe its length. Highlight the vocabulary that is used in their descriptions by writing each word on a blank index card. For instance, a child might say, "Your string is a little bit longer than my pencil." Focus on the word *longer* and show or create a new word card. Continue this process with other descriptive words as they are used. If words like *inches* and *centimeters* don't come up, you can decide whether or not you wish to introduce them.

4. Show the children the four different yarn lengths and let them know that in a few minutes you will give each of them a piece. Tell the students they will compare their pieces of yarn so that they will be able position themselves into one long line in order from the smallest yarn length to the largest.

5. Explain to the children that they will line up so that the children who have the longest pieces of yarn are at one end and those with the shortest are at the other end. Ask where the people who don't have the longest or the shortest yarn will go. Ask, "What will happen to the yarn as we look at our line?" In order to make sure that children understand the directions, ask several students to repeat them for the class before you pass out the yarn.

6. As you pass out the yarn, hold the pieces together toward the top as if you were drawing straws or holding a bouquet and let students select a piece without looking at the length. This will ensure random distribution. Try to arrange it so that there are about the same number of children with each yarn length.

7. Help the children compare their pieces of yarn with a partner. Then help the class get into an ordered line. Setting a time limit adds to the excitement. You might say, "When I get to zero counting backward from fifty, let's see if everyone can find his or her spot in the line!"

8. When the class line has been formed, most children will be next to someone with a piece of yarn that is the same length as their own. This could be a convenient way for children to cluster in small groups or partners for the upcoming yarn-length hunt. Have students hold their yarn pieces out in front of them so that the progression of length is easy to see.

9. Have students gather together and sit down while you explain the next phase of the lesson and introduce the recording sheet, if appropriate. Hold up a piece of yarn and ask the children to look around the room to help you find some things that are longer than the yarn that you are holding and some things that are shorter. Take your yarn over to the objects and compare the lengths or heights. Call attention to the end points of your yarn. Carefully position an end point to compare measurements and then show a counterexample by placing the end of

the yarn haphazardly. Discuss the results. If students will be using recording sheets, read it to them a couple of times, and then model the procedures for completion.

10. Tell the children that with their piece of yarn they are ready to participate in the length hunt, which means they will measure things in the classroom as you just did. Remind students to record their results on their recording sheets (if appropriate). You can decide if this will be a free exploration in the room or will be limited to a collection of objects in designated locations from which children can make their selections. (Children may decide to cluster together, but essentially this is an individual task.)

11. Begin the length hunt. As children find items to measure, talk with them about their results using comparative language. Observe how the children measure and the items that they select for making comparisons. These examples can be used for the processing discussion.

12. Set a time limit for the length hunt. Cue the class when there is a minute remaining and then again with thirty seconds left. Getting close to finishing time will very likely cause a flurry of activity and ensure that children complete the task and are ready to process their results.

13. When everyone is ready, call the children together. Ask each student to find a classmate who used a different-length piece of yarn. Ask partners to read and describe their recorded results. Show the class some of the items that were measured. Discuss the fact that an object, such as a chalkboard eraser, can be longer than one piece of yarn and at the same time shorter than another. As you illustrate this with the appropriate pieces of yarn, call attention to the end points of the yarn and the end points of the comparison object. Again, use mathematical vocabulary such as *longer, shorter,* and *equal to* as you compare the yarn and objects. Give children opportunities to practice this language as well by encouraging them to describe their comparisons.

Extension
◈ Use graph paper, rulers, or connecting cubes to establish conventional measurements of the yarn.

Ordering Bears and Things

Overview
This lesson uses the familiar bear characters from the favorite story *Goldilocks and the Three Bears,* but instead of just three bears, children work with twelve bears, each a different size, along with a corresponding set of bowls, chairs, and beds. (See Figure 1–2.)

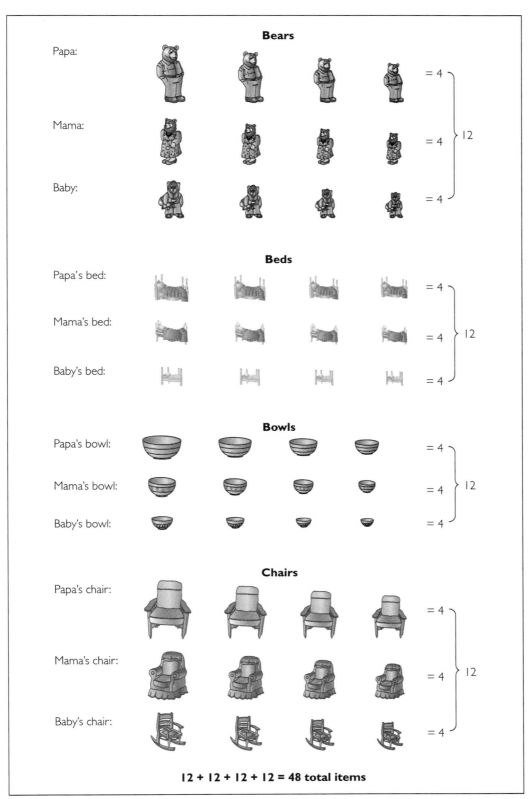

Figure 1–2 Ordering Bears and Things *Lesson*

As they place these items in order and create a one-to-one correspondence among them, children develop comparative and ordinal language and increase their understanding of number.

Materials

❖ *Goldilocks and the Three Bears*
❖ seriated sets of 3 bears, 3 bowls, 3 chairs, and 3 beds, 1 per pair of students, 4 sizes of each (see Blackline Masters)
❖ zip-top bags, 1 per pair of students
❖ 3-by-5-inch index cards, 10 to 20

Vocabulary: big, bigger, biggest, compare, eighth, eleventh, fifth, first, fourth, height, large, larger, largest, length, long, longer, longest, measure, ninth, order, second, seventh, short, shorter, shortest, sixth, small, smaller, smallest, tall, taller, tallest, tenth, third, twelfth

Instructions

1. Before class, prepare the sorting materials. Each set of materials should have a total of forty-eight pictures—twelve bears, twelve bowls, twelve chairs, and twelve beds, each of different sizes. To create a set, make a copy of each Blackline Master at four different sizes (using the copier's Reduce and Enlarge functions) on cardstock. Cut out the pictures and place them in a zip-top bag. Make enough sets so that children can work in pairs. (**Note:** For kindergartners, you may want to use just one item, such as the bears.)

2. Read *Goldilocks and the Three Bears* as an introduction to the lesson. Discuss similarities and differences between the characters, the bowls, the chairs, and the beds. Emphasize observations about the relative heights of the three bears. Reinforce comparative language, such as *bigger, smaller,* and so on. Create word cards, one word to an index card, to highlight the vocabulary you discuss.

3. Show the children a zip-top bag that contains a set of bears and accessories. Hold up the largest Mama Bear and the smallest Mama Bear and explain that you want to position all of the Mama Bears in order by height.

4. As you order the series of Mama Bears, think aloud about the placement of each piece. This gives the children an opportunity to observe the process of ordering and a context for using comparative language.

5. When you have ordered the Mama Bear pictures by height, play the *Missing Piece* game with a class volunteer. Explain that you are going to remove one of the bears and that the volunteer will have to guess where it belongs. Tell the class that you

will push the remaining bears back together so that the space where the missing bear belongs doesn't show. Ask for a volunteer. Tell your volunteer to look away while you remove a bear, and then push the remaining bears together to remove the space. Next, give the child the missing bear. While the child is looking for the correct spot to place the bear, verbalize what needs to be done. For instance, you might say: "We're looking for the spot where this bear is not too big and not too small. Is the bear in your hand bigger than this one? Is it smaller? Where does it belong so it fits just right?"

6. When the children understand the task of ordering the bears, introduce the accessories that go with the characters. Discuss the idea of placing the bowls, the chairs, and the beds in order. Model the use of comparative language as you show the materials. For example, "Here is my biggest Papa Bear and here is the biggest bowl" and "Here is the fourth chair and it goes by the fourth bed."

7. Pass out the sets of seriated pictures to partners. Designate places in the room where materials can be spread out so that children can sort and order the items. Explain that partners are to help one another order the sets and then play the *Missing Piece* game.

8. As you walk around the room and talk with children, discuss which pieces seem to be the easiest to place and which are the most difficult. Take the opportunity to do some assessing and play the *Missing Piece* game with individual students. It is natural for children to compare each bear one by one. When a student places missing pieces quickly, it is likely that this child is able to consider two criteria at once: (1) the missing piece in relation to all others that are smaller and (2) the piece in relation to all others that are larger. This shows that the child understands that a given number has its own distinct place in the order of numbers, being simultaneously smaller than some and larger than others.

9. After the materials have been put away, ask the children to consider some other things, besides the bears, that can be ordered by height. For instance, families can be ordered by height and groups of students can be ordered by height. Ask the children which would be easier to arrange in order by height—a family or a classroom full of children. Discuss the strategies that children used when ordering the bears, such as comparing two of them directly or selecting the largest or smallest and working from that extreme.

Extension

◈ Have the children look at rulers and make predictions about the height of a bear in centimeters and/or inches. Then have them measure and record the height of the various bears using the rulers.

◆ Name Trains

Overview

In this lesson, each child uses Snap Cubes and letter stickers to create a name train. Students compare the lengths of their name trains and determine how much longer some trains are than others.

Materials

- ❖ 1-inch Snap Cubes, enough for each letter of each student's first name
- ❖ dot stickers, enough for each letter of each student's first name
- ❖ chart of directions for activity (see Instruction 3)
- ❖ rulers, at least 1 per pair of students
- ❖ optional: *Name Trains* recording sheets, 1 per student (see Figure 1–3; see also Blackline Masters)

Vocabulary: combine, compare, equal, first, inch, last, length, longer, longest, ruler, same, shorter, shortest, total

Instructions

1. Create a context for the lesson by selecting the name of a familiar character, for instance, Franklin, if your students have heard some of the Franklin the turtle

Partner 1						
Partner 2						

The name _____ is **shorter.**

The name _____ is **longer.**

The name _____ is _____ cube(s) longer than _____.

Or

Both _____ and _____ are the **same length.**

Figure 1–3 Name Trains *Recording Sheet*

stories. Write the name in large print so that all of the children can see it. Have the children help you count the number of letters in the name and then connect that number of cubes, in this case, eight. Print the letters on eight small round stickers and place the letters on the cubes. Explain that you have built a name train for Franklin.

2. Ask the children to think about whether their first names will be longer, shorter, or the same length as Franklin's. Take an informal show of hands for each of the three possibilities. Have children record what they think in math notebooks or on a piece of paper that they can refer to later in the lesson.

3. Review and post the following directions:
   a. With cubes, make a name train that shows your name.
   b. Write the letters of your name on dot stickers and put them on the cubes.
   c. Compare your name train with your partner's. Decide whose name is shorter or longer or if they are the same length.
   d. Complete the recording sheet.

   Note: Omit Step 4 if not appropriate. Demonstrate how to record if appropriate.

4. Pair up the students and distribute the cubes and stickers.

5. After the students have completed the activity, ask the children to think back to their original comparisons with Franklin's name. Have several partners share the specific results of their conversations or recording sheets. Then ask questions like the following:
   • Does anyone have a name that is the same length as Franklin's? How long is it?
   • Who has the longest name? Is it longer than Franklin's? How many inches long is it?
   • Who has the shortest name in the class? What is the length of that name train?
   • Did any partners have the same-length names? Raise your hands if you and your partner had the same-length names. How long are your names? What do you think is the most common name length in the class?

6. Have students confirm that the cubes they are using are 1 inch long by taking a cube and measuring a side with a ruler. Discuss the starting point to make sure that children are reading the rulers accurately.

Extensions
◈ Have students combine and compare the lengths of their first and last names.
◈ Have the class estimate and determine the combined length of everyone's first name. Help the students place all of the name trains together into one long line.

◈ Match This Line

Overview

This partner activity involves one child drawing a straight line while the other attempts to replicate it. Both partners then measure their lines to see if they are indeed the same length.

Materials

◈ a selection of measuring tools such as Cuisenaire rods, cubes, string, rulers, and tape measures, enough so that several pairs of students can choose the same tool

Vocabulary: above, below, diagonal, down, horizontal, length, line, long, longer, longest, match, short, shorter, shortest, sideways, slanted, straight, up, vertical

Instructions

1. Begin the lesson by asking the children to define *straight line*. With a marker and a piece of paper, or an overhead transparency, draw a straight line that will measure about 5 centimeters long when displayed on an overhead projector. Ask the children to try to draw a line that is the same length as yours on a piece of scratch paper.

2. Use one of the measurement materials to determine the length of your original line. If your students are discussing standard units of measurement, you may wish to discuss significant vocabulary such as *inch* and *centimeter*.

3. Distribute measuring tools to the children, allowing them to choose what they want to work with. Students can use the same tool that you used or other tools that make sense to them. Ask children who are using the same tool that you did to measure their lines and compare the lengths with yours. Ask a few children to show their straight lines and share their methods of measuring.

4. Give each child a piece of paper and show the class how to fold the paper in half twice, once horizontally and once vertically, to create four separate sections. Ask the children to number the sections 1, 2, 3, and 4. Explain that students will be working with partners to play a game of *Match This Line* using the different sections of the paper.

    a. One partner draws a straight line, either vertically, horizontally, or diagonally, in Section 1 of his or her paper.
    b. The other partner tries to draw a straight line that is the same length and orientation in Section 1 of his or her paper.
    c. Both partners measure and compare their lines. (Demonstrate how to offset the two papers so that they are not directly aligned.)

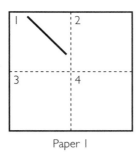

Paper 1

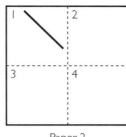

Paper 2

d. The second partner draws a line in Section 2 of his or her paper, and the game continues until the children have used all four sections.

5. Observe the children as they work and encourage the use of mathematical language. Reinforce and/or provide vocabulary as children compare the lengths of their line segments. For instance, a child might say, "My line is just a little bit longer." You could respond with "It looks like it's a bit less than a centimeter longer."

6. If there is time, children can turn their papers over and use the sections on the back to repeat the activity.

7. In a class discussion, ask children which type of line they drew more often—horizontal, vertical, or diagonal. Demonstrate the meaning of these words as you talk. Have the children look at their papers to see if there was a particular type of line segment that was more challenging to reproduce than any other.

8. Ask several partners to share their methods of measurement and why they chose them. Find out how many children used cubes, Cuisenaire rods, string, tape measures, and rulers. Ask about the reasoning behind those choices. For example, a child might say, "We used cubes and we liked them because they were easy to line up and count," or "We used a tape measure and we liked it because there are numbers already on it, but it was hard to tell what all those little lines were for."

9. Ask children which measurement tool they have the greatest confidence in and why. Which seemed to be the most accurate? Why? Which tool would they choose to do this activity the next time? Why?

Extensions
◈ Allow children to use curved lines; they can measure and compare using yarn or string.
◈ Have children create small figures or symbols, like letters, for comparisons.

◈ Around the Shape

Overview

Students use a variety of nonstandard units of measure such as toothpicks, cubes, Cuisenaire rods (one size at a time), and paper clips to measure the distance around geometric shapes. After making predictions, children measure and record the distance around their shapes. They then compare their results to determine which of the shapes has the greatest perimeter, or distance around.

Materials

❖ *Around the Shape* recording sheets of the following polygons: square, rectangle, triangle, and trapezoid, at least 1 per student (see Blackline Masters)

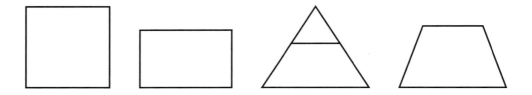

❖ measurement units such as toothpicks, cubes, paper clips, and Cuisenaire rods (grouped by color), enough so that several students can select the same material

Vocabulary: all, around, between, distance, gaps, half, length, long, longer, longest, next to, part, perimeter, short, shorter, shortest, side, spaces, width

Instructions

1. Introduce the activity by playing a guessing game about polygons that is similar to I spy and highlights some vocabulary that will be used during the activity. For instance, you might start with "I'm thinking of a shape that has four sides and each of those sides is exactly the same length" or "I'm thinking of a shape that can have different-length sides, but there are always three sides." Continue the game until you have introduced each shape that the children will use in the activity. After each set of clues, reveal and name the shape that you are describing.

2. Explain to the children that they will be measuring around every side of a shape. Show the students the possible measurement units that they will choose from. Select a shape and one of the measurement units, like toothpicks, and ask students to make predictions about how many toothpicks will be needed to measure the distance of one side of the shape. After hearing the predictions, model measuring with the toothpicks, and compare the answer with their predictions. Next, ask,

"How many toothpicks will be needed to measure the distance around the whole shape?" Once again, after hearing the predictions, measure. Place toothpicks along the remaining sides of the shape. Together with the class, count the toothpicks to determine the perimeter, or distance around the shape. Discuss what to do if the measurement of a side does not work out evenly. For instance, suppose two toothpicks and about half of a third one fit along the side of a shape. Show the class that the length of the side can be recorded as $2\frac{1}{2}$. Explain that it is important to place the measurement objects end-to-end and not leave gaps between them.

3. Distribute a recording sheet (a copy of each shape) to each child. Direct each child to pick a shape and a measurement unit and then measure the sides of the shape and record. Individual students who have time may measure more than one shape using several different measurement units.

4. At the end of the lesson, partner each student with a classmate who measured the same shape so that they can compare their results. After students have had an opportunity to share their recorded information, have them talk about their experiences with the whole group by asking questions like these:

   • Who measured ———— (name a particular shape)?
   • Did you get exactly the same results as your partner? (Ask for some examples.)
   • Did any partners get different results? Why do you think this happened?
   • Does it make a difference if you and your partner used different materials? Why?
   • Does it matter how you place the measuring units? Can there be spaces between them? Can they overlap?
   • Did anyone get answers that weren't exact? What did you do?
   • Which shape had the longest distance around? Why do you think so? Is there a way that we could check to make sure?

5. Post several recording sheets as examples in the room.

Extension

❖ In addition to the children's suggestions for determining which shape has the longest perimeter, consider the following. Use string to measure around the shapes. Straighten each string, keeping track of which shape's perimeter it represents, and compare the strings to see which is the longest.

 Dots

Overview

In this activity, children have an opportunity to develop geometric and measurement skills. After drawing and connecting four dots with a straightedge to create a quadrilateral, children measure and compare the lengths of its sides.

Materials

◈ large drawings of quadrilaterals, such as a parallelogram, a rectangle, a trapezoid, an irregular quadrilateral, and a rhombus, about 5

◈ paper circles, 5 inches in diameter, 4

◈ a ball or skein of yarn

◈ rulers or straightedges, 1 per student

◈ centimeter or 1-inch cubes or tiles, about 15 per student

◈ optional: blank overhead transparency

Vocabulary: above, below, beside, closest, compare, corner, distance, dot, farthest, inside, left, length, long, longer, longest, measure, minimum, next to, rectangle, right, same, shape, short, shorter, shortest, side, space, straight line, top

Instructions

1. Explain to the class that you want to position the paper circles on the board so that they are not in a straight line and that at least three fingers can fit between any two of them. When you have all four paper circles arranged and taped in place, ask the children to consider which two are the closest together and which are the farthest apart. Encourage descriptive language such as *above, below,* and *next to.* Cut the yarn to create line segments from one paper circle to another. Compare the distance between the circles by comparing the lengths of the cut yarn. Tape the yarn segments to the paper circles to form a quadrilateral. Label the longest line *L* and the shortest line *S.*

2. Explain to the children that this activity will involve drawing four dots and connecting them to make a shape like you did with the circles and the yarn. Tell them that their shape does not need to look like one of the rectangles in the *Around the Shape* lesson (page 14), but it does need to have four corners (the dots) and four sides. (Show examples of some quadrilaterals such as a trapezoid and a rhombus.)

3. Model the procedure that the children will use. On the overhead projector or board, draw four dots that are not in a row and when connected will form an irregular quadrilateral. Place a ruler on two of the dots and draw a line to connect them. Repeat this process until all four dots are connected and a closed figure, or four-sided-shape, has been created.

4. Next, demonstrate how to find the length of each side of your shape. Use centimeter cubes or tiles. Think out loud as you carefully place the cubes next to one another, leaving no gaps between them. Explain that you are creating a line, or a path, with your cubes from one dot to another. Discuss ideas to help the children record parts of cubes such as $\frac{1}{2}$. For example: "I have some extra space left over here; what could I do? If it's just a little bit, don't worry about it. If it's about half, show it

as one-half, or if there is another amount like three-fourths that makes sense, use that. Label sides with the number of cubes that were needed to go from one dot to another."

5. Pass out the cubes or tiles, some blank 8½-by-11-inch paper, and the rulers or straightedges. Remind the children that they are to

   • draw four dots, not in a line, and at least three fingers apart;
   • connect them to form a four-sided shape;
   • measure each side of the shape using cubes or tiles; and
   • write the number of units used next to the side being measured. (See Figure 1–4.)

6. As you walk around and observe the children, help those who are having trouble drawing straight lines. Make a note of children who seem to be unconcerned about spaces between the cubes as they position the materials from dot to dot. Assist students as they record information about the length of each line.

7. As children complete the task, discuss their measurements. After the lesson, lead a whole-class discussion, asking questions like "Were any two of your lines the same length? How long was your longest line? How long was your shortest line? What was the difference between the two? How many more tiles or cubes did you use in your longest line than in your shortest?"

Extensions

❖ Have each child incorporate his or her four-sided shape into a picture or scene.
❖ Change the number of dots or the size of the paper.

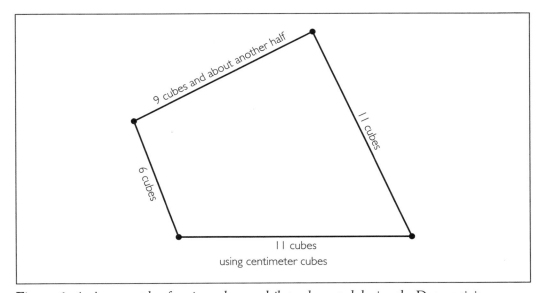

Figure 1–4 *An example of an irregular quadrilateral created during the Dots activity.*

❖ Have students use centimeter- or inch-grid paper and place the dots where the lines intersect.

❖ Have children experiment, using string or yarn, with measuring curved versus straight lines.

Growing Things

Overview

In this lesson, students learn about the process of planting seeds. The class keeps track of the length of time it takes for seeds to germinate and then of the weekly growth of the seedlings.

Materials

❖ children's literature books such as *From Seed to Plant,* by Gail Gibbons (1991), *Sunflower,* by Miela Ford (1995), and *The Tiny Seed,* by Eric Carle (1990)

❖ sunflower or bean seeds, avocado pits, and amaryllis bulbs, a variety, at least 16

❖ small plastic cups for seed samples, 8

❖ large transparent bag of potting soil

❖ pots with saucers, 6 inches in diameter, 6 or 7

❖ centimeter cubes and/or centimeter paper strips, 1 per student

❖ *Growing Things* recording sheet, 1 per student (see Blackline Masters)

❖ class calendar

Vocabulary: amaryllis, avocado, bulb, centimeter, germinate, growth, height, inch, length of time, measure, pit, predict, seed, sunflower, tall

Instructions

1. Before the lesson begins, number four of the pots 1 through 4 and arrange the planting materials so that students will be able to watch as you plant the seeds. Prepare and plant two or three extra pots in case of unforeseen events such as spills or lack of germination. Place some samples of the seeds in the eight plastic cups.

2. Begin the lesson by reading a story listed in the "Materials" section. Ask the children to describe what they understand about the relationship between seeds and plants. Pass around the small cups with the seed samples so that the children can examine and compare them. Tell the children the name of the plant that will grow from each seed and identify whether each seed is considered a seed, a bulb, or a pit.

3. Describe the planting process as you position the seeds in the four numbered containers. Place a saucer under each container and water each pot. Explain to the children that you will place the seed pots in a sunny location and water them regularly.

4. Ask the class to consider questions such as these: "Do you think that a bigger seed will take longer to germinate or turn into a plant than a smaller seed? Do you think that more sunlight will make a difference? Do you think that talking to a plant will help? What do you think helps a plant grow from a seed?" Have students make predictions about when plants will germinate. When the various plants do begin to emerge, mark the pot numbers on the classroom calendar.

5. Show the children the recording sheet and explain that everyone in the class will work with a small group to keep track of one of the four plants (see Figure 1–5). Tell them that each week the children who are assigned to a particular seed pot will draw and measure any changes in that particular plant. Divide your class into four groups and assign each group to a certain plant.

6. Each week, provide a time for students to check their plants and update their recordings. Introduce the centimeter cubes and/or centimeter paper strips. Have a whole-class discussion about how to use these tools to get the most accurate information about the height of the plants without damaging them. Have children use the recording sheets to draw visuals and record growth.

Name:	I am observing seed number:	
Week I	Week 2	Week 3
Week 4	Week 5	Week 6

Figure 1–5 Growing Things *Recording Sheet*

7. At the end of six weeks, have each group create a large display of its plant's growth from Week 1 to Week 6. Have groups share these displays with the class, and then post them in the classroom.

Extension

❖ Have students plant their own seeds to take home along with recording sheets and centimeter strips.

 Measure the Classroom

Overview

After reading *The Line Up Book*, by Marisabina Russo, the class makes predictions about how many items could be lined up across the classroom. Children work in pairs to measure the width of the room using nonstandard units and report on their findings to the class. When the results are shared, issues involving unit size and quantity of measurement objects surface.

Materials

❖ *The Line Up Book*, by Marisabina Russo (1992)
❖ a variety of nonstandard measurement objects such as books, pencils, paper clips, clothespins, cubes, plastic links, Cuisenaire rods, and blocks, enough of each to span the width of your classroom
❖ optional: pad of chart paper

Vocabulary: across, fewer, in between, length, line, long, longer, longest, more, next to, object, predictions, same amount, short, shorter, shortest, space between, straight, width

Instructions

1. Show the class *The Line Up Book*, read the title, and ask the children if the title gives them a clue about what the book might be about. After reading the story, ask some questions like the following:

• As the little boy lined things up on his way to the kitchen, what things did he use?
• What did he use the most of?
• What was the biggest object (or thing) that he used?
• How many objects do you think he had in his line?

- What could the little boy do if he wanted to actually measure his room instead of just making a line to the kitchen?
- Would it matter how he placed the objects or not? Why?

2. To create a list of objects in the classroom that might be used to measure the distance across the room, ask, "What are some things that we could use to measure our room here at school?" Write the children's suggestions on the board or chart paper.

3. Use a desk or another convenient surface to take some quick measurements and give the children a chance to make predictions and see results. For instance, you might place crayons across the desk, counting as you go. Next, use a different-size object, like cubes. Since small objects will require more counting, discuss ways that might help you keep track of larger numbers, such as inserting a different-colored cube each time you reach ten. This is also an opportunity to make a point of the significance of the careful placement of the objects, end-to-end without gaps.

4. Have the children make some predictions about how many pencils would be needed to make a line from one side of the room to the other. Jot down on chart paper or the board some of their guesses. Do the same for a few of the remaining suggested objects. Ask, "Would it take more cubes or more books to go from one side of the room to the other? Why? More cubes or more pencils? More pencils or more paper clips?"

5. Show children the materials that you've collected to measure the width of the classroom and invite the children to work with a partner to create a line of objects from one side of the room to the other. Remind the students that they can't mix and match the items; they must use the same item for the entire distance. Have each child draw a picture of his or her measurement process and record the number of objects that it took to span the room.

6. During the next class period, select some students to explain what they used to measure the room and how many objects were needed. Ask if there are two groups who used the same type of object to create a line across the room. Compare the counts. If the two reports are not exactly the same, discuss possible reasons for the differences. Record the results from all partners on the board or chart paper; for example: Jenny and Emily used _pencils_; it took _50_.

7. Ask the children to think about possible explanations for the different numbers that were reported. Refer to the counts that you've recorded to point out that the size of the measurement unit influences the count.

8. End the lesson by having the children help you arrange the various nonstandard units that were used to measure the room in order by length.

Extensions

❧ Have children predict and investigate the classroom's length as opposed to its width.

❧ Collaborate with the physical education teacher to have the children use some materials from the physical education program to measure the gym.

❧ Ask children to measure the length of their bedroom or the length of a route to their kitchen.

 ## Round and Round

Overview

After putting a collection of jar and bottle lids in order by size, students measure the circumference of the lids with string and compare the lengths of the strings.

Materials

❧ round lids from jars and bottles of varied sizes, 1 per student plus 2 or 3 extras

❧ paper sack large enough to hold all the lids

❧ string, about 12 inches long, 1 piece per student

❧ thick piece of yarn, about 12 inches long

❧ two-sided tape or masking tape

Vocabulary: alike, around, beginning, big, bigger, biggest, circle, circumference, compare, conjectures, counting words, distance, identical, length, less, long, longer, longest, more, most, order, similar, size, small, smaller, smallest

Instructions

1. Before class, put all the lids into the paper sack. To begin the lesson, jiggle the sack. As you shake the bag, explain to the children that the things inside the bag are alike in some ways, but not identical. Invite the children to speculate about what might be inside the bag. After discussing some possibilities, have each child reach inside and take a lid. If you have time, have each student write or tape his or her name on the lid.

2. Ask pairs of students who are seated near each other to describe two ways that their lids are the same and two ways that they are different. Then, as a whole class, discuss size attributes and highlight mathematical vocabulary such as *same size, smaller, larger,* and *compared with.*

3. Have the students speculate about who might have the very smallest lid. Have that child place the lid so that everyone can see it. Then ask, "Who has the next largest lid?" or "Who has a lid just a little bigger than this one?" Have that child

place his or her lid next to the first lid. Get consensus from the class that the lid is slightly larger before going on. Again ask, "Now who has the next largest?" and continue the process until all the lids have been placed in a row and ordered by size. If two lids appear to be the same size, have the class agree upon how they should be positioned; for example, they could be stacked or one could be placed above or below another.

4. After the lids have been placed in one long ordered row, pose this question: "How can we determine if one lid is smaller than another without picking them up and comparing them directly? "Discuss the children's ideas about making indirect comparisons. Next, explain that they will be using yarn as a measuring tool to compare two lids.

5. Show the children your thick piece of yarn. Tell the class that you intend to wrap the yarn around a bottle lid so that you can measure the distance around it. Explain that the distance around a circle has a special math name called *circumference*.

6. Use one of the extra lids from the lid collection. Ask the students to predict how long the string will need to be in order to go around the lid exactly once. Make a cutting motion with your fingers to indicate some possible points that match their predictions.

7. Wrap the yarn around the lid and have a partner assist you as you cut the yarn at the point where it meets the beginning of the yarn after going all the way around the lid exactly once. Discuss the importance of being as accurate as possible when cutting the string. Explain that partners need to work together to hold and cut the string carefully.

8. Have children retrieve their lids from the row of lids. Pass out the measuring strings and scissors. Encourage partners to assist one another as they place and cut the string to measure the circumference of their lids.

9. When this task has been completed, the class will have a set of circumference strings to match the class set of lids. Have the children get back together as a large group. Ask the students if they think that the largest circle has the longest string and the smallest circle has the shortest string. Have children explain their reasoning. Once again mention that the distance around a circle is called a circumference. Ask the child holding the string with the longest circumference to hold it up and then to hold the lid up as well.

10. Next, have the children organize themselves in one long line spanning the classroom from longest string to shortest string. Ask them to bring their lids along with them as well.

11. Once the class is in line, ask them to hold up their circumference strings for comparison. With their other hands, have them hold out their lids.

12. Ask children to explain what they notice. Make a list of their remarks and have the children leave the lids and strings arranged in order so that you can create a display to remind them of their work.

13. Using two-sided tape or masking tape, select a variety of sizes and display each selected lid along with its circumference string. Indicate that the larger the lid, the longer the string.

Extensions
❖ Have children add to the lid collection, and make this measurement activity a learning center.
❖ Have students determine the length of the circumference strings in centimeters and/or inches.
❖ Have children look for circles in the room, for example, the trash can or the base of the class globe. They can measure the circumference and translate it into standard units of measurement.

Inch by Inch

Overview
Leo Lionni's book *Inch by Inch* provides an entertaining introduction to a familiar standard measurement unit. In the story, an inchworm proves that he can measure anything from a robin's tail, to a flamingo's neck, to a heron's legs, to the entire length of a hummingbird. This lesson helps children to understand length, width, and distance as they measure pictures of birds.

Materials
❖ *Inch by Inch*, by Leo Lionni (1995)
❖ 1-inch tiles or cubes, 20 per student
❖ pictures of birds, 2 per student (see Figure 1–6; see also Blackline Masters)

Vocabulary: all, between, distance, dot, end point, fraction, from . . . to . . . , height, length, long, longer, longest, measure, part, short, shorter, shortest

Instructions

1. Read the story *Inch by Inch* to the class. Discuss the inchworm's predicament and the clever way that he solved his problem.

Figure 1–6 *Examples of bird drawings used in the* Inch by Inch *activity.*

2. Ask the children if they have seen worms outside, and discuss their lengths. Using one side of an inch square tile as a guide, draw a line segment to show how long an inchworm would actually be. Explain that each side of the tile is an inch long.

3. Talk about some of the things that the inchworm measured in the story. Show the children one of the bird pictures that will be used in the activity and talk about what measurements, such as length and width, could be taken using 1-inch tiles. Discuss some of the challenges that would be involved in measuring the bird, such as where to begin and end, what to use to measure the distance, and how to record what you've measured.

4. Choose a dimension such as height to measure with the tiles. Model creating two points to show where the height begins and where it ends. Draw a line between the two points, and then explain that this is where you intend to place the tiles. Place the tiles carefully so that they are touching, leaving no spaces between them. Have the children help you count as you position the tiles along the line. Discuss what would happen if spaces were left between the tiles.

5. Ask the children what they might do if the 1-inch tiles do not fit perfectly along the line. Discuss estimating to the nearest tile. Demonstrate writing a number that will indicate part of an inch, such as $\frac{1}{2}$.

6. Show the children the various bird pictures to be measured. Have students select one or two pictures to measure. After selecting their pictures, students can work on this activity independently or with a partner.

7. Review the procedures:
   - Decide upon the direction that you wish to measure your bird.
   - Make two points on the bird to show the end points of the distance to be measured.
   - Draw a line from one end point to the other.
   - Position the tiles between the two dots and along the line, leaving no space between them.
   - Count the tiles.
   - Record the results on your picture.

8. Circulate while the children work and take note of how accurately the children are managing the tiles. Encourage them to talk to you about their work by asking questions about how they decided to position their dots. Listen for vocabulary such as *length*, *width*, and *height*. Observe how students place tiles on their lines and how they deal with remainders.

9. When the children have finished working, discuss their results and the challenges that they encountered. Have a few volunteers share their recordings. Discuss whether or not the tiles fit in between the end points exactly. Ask if anyone had a picture that used the same number of tiles from point to point as another student. Compare the pictures and discuss whether or not the measured distances appear to be the same length.

10. Post the pictures in the room so that the children have a chance to look carefully at the variety of measurements that were taken.

Extensions
❖ Have children reuse the same pictures but measure in a different direction. It helps to mark the end points with a different color than the first set of points.
❖ Have students use centimeters instead of inches to measure the birds.

 Partner Pictures

Overview
In this lesson, partners use two identical sets of stickers to create matching scenes or "twin" pictures. Partners attempt to position their stickers in exactly the same places on their papers and then use measurement tools to help them determine if they have done so.

Materials

❖ sets of five matching stickers, 2 per pair of students

❖ tools for measuring, such as paper centimeter strips, paper inch strips, or cube sticks, at least 1 per student (see Blackline Masters)

❖ crayons or colored pencils, enough for the class to share

Vocabulary: above, below, beside, between, bottom, centimeters, closer, different, distance, farther, left, matching, measure, near, next to, right, same, side, top

Instructions

1. Prior to the lesson, prepare two twin pictures using stickers. Position and place five stickers in the same locations on two pieces of paper and then determine a setting or scene for the pictures and decorate each the same way.

2. Begin the lesson by drawing two matching rectangles on the board. Invite a volunteer to come up and place an X somewhere in one of the rectangles. Tell the class that you want to position an X in the other rectangle in the same spot. Ask children to talk to each other for a minute or two about how to find the correct spot in the empty rectangle. Use some of their ideas to position the second X. For example, a student may suggest checking to see how far the first X is from the top of the rectangle and matching that distance in the second rectangle. Another student might suggest checking to see how far the X is from the left side of the rectangle. Use these types of suggestions to introduce the measurement tools. For example, demonstrate the use of cube sticks or paper strips to position the X on the second rectangle.

3. Ask your student volunteer to help position a second symbol in the rectangles, such as an O. This time, the X can also be used to help determine the spot for the O. Discuss various ways to check the accuracy of the position: from the top, the bottom, the sides, and the X.

4. Explain to the class that with a partner everyone will create twin pictures using paper rectangles (blank $8\frac{1}{2}$-by-11-inch paper), and stickers. Show the children the pictures you made earlier and the sets of matching stickers. Remind the class of the examples using Xs and Os and then ask students to restate some of the measurement strategies. Record their ideas, such as measure from the top, measure from the sides, and measure from other points. Make sure that everyone has access to measurement tools.

5. Pair up the children, pass out two sets of stickers and two sheets of paper to each pair, and set them to work. First, Partner A places five stickers on his piece of paper. Then Partner B tries to place her set of stickers in the same positions on her

paper, with Partner A's help. Give children ample time to finish this part of the activity.

6. After the children have successfully placed their stickers, have them use crayons or colored pencils to create scenes. Students may choose to create different pictures or settings for their stickers. That could generate some interesting discussion about the perception of distance.

7. During a whole-class discussion, ask students if the placement of some stickers made it easier to match another person's picture. Ask: "If stickers were close to the outside edges, was it easier to match their positions than if they were closer to the center? Was it more difficult if they were closer to the center? Was it easier if you had stickers clustered together or far apart from each other? Were you able to accurately make twin pictures? Are the measurements fairly close?"

8. Put the pictures and the measurement tools on display. (See Figures 1–7 and 1–8.)

Extensions

❖ Increase the level of complexity of this task by introducing more features that students need to match. For example, have students create matching maps with features like rivers, roadways, and mountains.

Figure 1–7 *Tony placed his stickers first in the* Partner Pictures *activity.*

Figure 1–8 *Camille used cubes to measure from the outside edges to position her stickers. Then she drew her picture.*

 Foot Race

Overview

Foot Race is a dice game designed to build children's mental image of 1-inch units. It helps students develop the understanding that twelve consecutive inches equal one foot. Play requires students to roll a die and connect the corresponding number of 1-inch cubes until they get to 1 foot.

Materials

- ❧ rulers or inch strips (see Blackline Masters), 1 per student
- ❧ number dice, 1 per student
- ❧ 1-inch cubes, 12 per student
- ❧ demonstration objects such as a paper clip, an eraser, and a book
- ❧ 3-by-5-inch index cards, at least 5
- ❧ optional: *Foot Race* recording sheets, 1 per student (see Blackline Masters)

Vocabulary: combine, compare, connect, cube, dice, die, exactly, foot, inch, least, most, possible, repeat, roll

Instructions

1. Show the class a ruler and a 1-inch cube. Ask the students to share what they know and/or notice about these objects. Using the 3-by-5-inch index cards, create word cards, writing one word on each card: *ruler, inch,* and *foot.* As you read the words aloud, explain that inches and feet are units of measure that people can use to describe how long something is. Cubes and rulers are tools that help people count and keep track of inches and feet. Discuss real-life connections such as buying shoes or measuring a window to see how long a curtain rod should be.

2. Hold up some of the demonstration objects like a paper clip, a book, and an eraser. Ask the children to consider whether each object is closer in length to an inch or a foot. Check the predictions using a ruler and/or cubes.

3. Introduce *Foot Race* by explaining that the game requires players to keep track of inches by connecting 1-inch cubes until they reach a foot.

4. Demonstrate rolling a die, counting out the corresponding number of cubes, and connecting them. Repeat this process until you have built a tower that is a foot high. Explain that players do not need an exact roll of 12 to finish. The recording sheets will reinforce the understanding that 12 inches is the exact number of inches in a foot. (See Figure 1–9.)

5. Provide each student with twelve cubes, a number die, and a 1-foot strip or ruler, along with a pencil and a recording sheet, if appropriate for your students. Ask the children if they are likely to roll a total of exactly 12 to go out. Discuss the reasons for their predictions. As students roll their die, have them place cubes directly on top of the ruler so that they can see the relationship between inches and a foot.

6. Set a predetermined amount of time to play the game. Circulate while the children work, observing and discussing their progress. As you interact, you can assess students' counting accuracy and efficiency.

7. After the class plays the game for the designated amount of time, ask the children to put their materials away and prepare to discuss their results. Begin the processing by having the children first show you with their fingers about how long an inch is and then show with their hands the length of a foot. Determine whether anyone finished the game with exactly 12 inches and discuss what those students rolled. Next ask the people who went beyond 12 on their final roll to raise their hands. Discuss some reasons for these results.

Game 1
I rolled:
_____   _____
_____   _____
_____   _____
_____   _____
_____   _____
_____

I had exactly 12 when I went out.   Yes   or   No

Game 2
I rolled:
_____   _____
_____   _____
_____   _____
_____   _____
_____   _____
_____

I had exactly 12 when I went out.   Yes   or   No

Game 3
I rolled:
_____   _____
_____   _____
_____   _____
_____   _____
_____   _____
_____

I had exactly 12 when I went out.   Yes   or   No

Figure 1–9 Foot Race *Recording Sheet*

8. If there is time, give some examples of combinations from game results and ask the children if the numbers combine to make exactly one foot or more than one foot. For example: $5 + 5 + 5 = 12$? $4 + 6 + 2 = 12$? $4 + 5 + 6 = 12$? $6 + 6 = 12$?

Extensions

❧ Have students count up the number of games they have completed and make some guesses about how long that number of feet would look like. Ask if that length would fit in your room, the hallway, the playground, or the gym.

❧ Have the children use rulers end-to-end or tape measures to confirm the accuracy of the distances in feet that were reported during the class session of *Foot Race*.

❧ Ask the children to think about some of the combinations of numbers that could be rolled to go out on exactly 12. Write those equations on the board. For instance: $6 + 6 = 12, 2 + 5 + 5 = 12$.

❧ Have students use two dice instead of one. See how many feet the class has accumulated after ten minutes.

❧ Have students use centimeter rulers instead of inch rulers during the lesson.

Sticker Pictures

Overview

In this lesson, children incorporate stickers into theme-related pictures that they have drawn. Once their stickers are positioned, they choose from a variety of measurement tools to determine the distance from one sticker to another. The children then compare the distances.

Materials

◈ stickers, preferably tactile foam, 3 per student

◈ crayons or markers, enough for the class to share

◈ selection of measuring tools such as 1-inch or 1-centimeter cubes, rulers, strips of paper, and string, enough for each pair of students

◈ 3-by-5-inch index cards, 3

◈ optional: chart paper

Vocabulary: above, below, beneath, between, bottom, closest, distance, farthest, left, length, longest, measure, middle, right, shortest, top, under

Instructions

1. Prior to the lesson, prepare word cards for *distance*, *length*, and *measure*. Put each word on an index card.

2. Begin the lesson by explaining to the class that each student will make a picture using three stickers and` then measure the distance between the stickers. You may want to use stickers that go along with a particular topic. For example, if you are involved in a unit on butterflies, your stickers could relate to that theme.

3. Model the activity. Show the children the three stickers you have chosen. Draw a picture to provide a suitable background scene, for instance, flowers, clouds, and trees.

4. Place your three stickers on the drawing so that the distances are dissimilar. Ask the children to describe what they notice about the placement of the stickers. On chart paper or on the board, where everyone can see, record the mathematical vocabulary as the children use comparative terms such as *closer*, *farther*, *longer*, *shorter*, and so on. (See Figure 1–10.)

5. Display the word cards. Show and discuss the measurement tools that children will choose from. Select a measurement tool and measure the distances between your stickers, demonstrating how to count and compare.

6. Invite the children to select three stickers, make their own pictures on blank 8½-by-11-inch paper with crayons or markers, and use a measurement tool of their choice

Figure 1–10 *Samantha created a drawing, placed her stickers, and then measured the distances with cm cubes.*

to quantify the distances between their stickers. Have them record their measurements at the bottom of their pictures or between the stickers. (**Note:** Tactile foam stickers make it especially easy to judge the edge of each sticker as the children do their measuring.)

7. Post these questions in a place where all can see:
   - What is the longest distance between two of your stickers?
   - What is the shortest distance between two of your stickers?
   - How do you know? What did you use to measure the distance?

   If students are ready for more complexity, follow up with questions about the actual lengths, such as:
   - How much longer is the distance between stickers (A and B) than (B and C)?
   - Is there another way that you could check this measurement?

8. Have partners discuss these questions with each other. Walk around the room and listen to their conversations. When everyone is ready, ask a few children to share their results with the class. Choose examples that feature different measuring tools. Help focus students' attention on the placement of measurement materials. Demonstrate a situation where part of a cube, for example, is on the line and part is not. Discuss how this part could be counted.

Extensions

❖ Allow students to use more stickers and/or larger pieces of paper.

❖ Have children measure the stickers on someone else's paper to check that student's results. Do partners get the same results? If not, why not?

❖ Have children dictate their observations about the relative distances between their stickers, and type them below the pictures. Put them on display.

❖ Change the instructions so that children try to have all of the stickers the same distance apart.

❖ Have the class create a mural of stickers and then figure out the farthest distance between two stickers.

 Double or Half

Overview

Children have long been fascinated by characters of extreme size. From Stuart Little to the giant in *Jack and the Beanstalk,* size is often a featured aspect of storytelling. In this lesson children explore the concepts of doubling and halving by comparing different-size pictures of an imaginary little boy named George.

Materials

❖ *George Shrinks,* by William Joyce (1985)

❖ set of five pictures of George that gradually increase in size, 1 per pair of students (see Blackline Masters)

❖ 3-by-5-inch index cards, 2

❖ measuring tools such as cubes, tiles, string, rulers, grid paper, and Cuisenaire rods, enough for each pair of students

Vocabulary: big, bigger, biggest, double, enormous, half, height, length, long, longer, longest, original, regular, shrinks, small, smaller, smallest, tall, taller, tallest, tiny, twice

Instructions

1. Before class, create two word cards. On one index card write *half;* on the other, write *double.*

2. Read *George Shrinks* to the class. Discuss what it would be like to be *impossibly little* or *enormous.* Encourage the children to identify heights by thinking about questions like "What if you were as big as a building? What if you were as tiny as a butterfly?"

3. Show the children the original picture of George (the 4-inch version with a G on his shirt). Then show them the other four pictures of George. Ask the children what they notice about these pictures. Acknowledge that they are different sizes

and explain that two of the pictures have a special relationship to the original picture. One of the pictures is actually *half* (show the word card) the height of the original George and another is *double* (show the word card) the height of the original George. (See Figure 1–11.)

4. Discuss the meanings of the words *double* and *half*. Demonstrate the definitions using tangible examples made with plastic links or paper clips, paper, and/or string.

5. Explain to the children that in today's math lesson they will work with a partner to decide *which* George is half the height and which one is double the height of the George with the G on his shirt. Show the children the tools that are available, such

Figure 1–11 *Set of five George characters for the* Double or Half *activity.*

as Cuisenaire rods, grid paper, rulers, string, tiles, and cubes. Then provide time for children to talk in small groups about how to solve the problem. Ask volunteers from different groups to share their thinking with the whole class.

6. Provide each pair with a set of the five George characters and have them select the measuring tools of their choice. Students can cut the characters out during the lesson if that is a strategy that comes up. Set a time limit for solving the problem and check in periodically to give students a sense of how much time remains. For example, tell the students that they will have twenty minutes to complete their work.

7. When the time is up, call the class together and ask the children to discuss their efforts. Students may say things like, "We used cubes to measure and we found that the smallest George was two inches, the middle one was four inches, and the tallest one was eight inches," or "We used string, and the littlest one looked much smaller than the biggest one." Record the statements as students share. Help children articulate their ideas about halving and doubling by demonstrating them with the measuring tools. Reinforce the ideas of *doubling height*, *twice as big*, and *half* by writing the words and emphasizing their mathematical language.

Extensions
◈ Revisit the lesson and have children use a different measurement tool than they did during their initial exploration of the problem.
◈ Children can each create their own character using 1-inch grid paper. After they have drawn and measured the character, they can create another that is twice as tall or double in length. Ask the children if doubling the length is the same thing as doubling the height. How are length and height related?

Time

Introduction

Children are continuously affected by time. At the point that kindergartners begin school, routines and schedules are already shaping their lives. And yet from a child's perspective, time is elastic and vague. We're all familiar with phrases such as: Are we there yet? How much longer? and Just a minute! We can help children make sense of concepts of time by building on their existing understandings and offering repeated meaningful experiences.

This chapter includes a short lesson about using recurring routines as a means of addressing this need for repetition. One aspect of telling time that confuses many children is distinguishing between the two hands on the clock and their functions. Centuries ago, the general public used only the hour hand to tell time. Some lessons in this chapter use a similar premise and provide opportunities for students to develop understandings about hours and minutes separately. Instead of focusing attention on comparing the length of the clock's hands, the lessons focus on the patterns of time that the hands create.

Patterns and sequences of time ranging from days and nights to weeks, months, years, and seasons are included in lessons that are presented in a variety of contexts. Students estimate, collect data, and represent their thinking in tasks that involve physical activity, children's literature, and outdoor science observations.

Recurring Routines

Overview
Building routines related to time into your classroom schedule helps children understand time in contexts that are connected to their lives. The following are ways to highlight the sequences of predictable events and specific times of the day.

Materials
◈ bulletin board display calendar
◈ old calendar illustrations, postcards, and seasonal magazine pictures

- birthday and special dates time line
- household flip calendar
- cutouts for the bulletin board display calendar, 10 different shapes (made with an Ellison machine or commercial shapes), each in 5 different colors
- sixty-minute clock faces, 1 per student (see Blackline Masters)
- paper clock faces, 3 inches in diameter, and tape or adhesive magnets (see Blackline Masters)
- kitchen and sand timers, 1 each
- manipulative clocks, 1 per student
- optional: chart paper

Vocabulary: April, August, day, December, February, Friday, future, January, June, July, March, May, Monday, month, nonfiction, November, October, past, pattern, predict, routine, Saturday, September, Sunday, Thursday, Tuesday, Wednesday, week, year

Instructions

Developing Understandings About Months

Use old calendar illustrations, postcards, or seasonal magazine pictures to create a display that includes each month of the year. Display the sequence of months on available wall space in your room. Beneath each month, list the dates of class members' birthdays along with special days such as conference days, holidays, and school events like book sales and bake sales. New events can be added to the list as the year progresses. (See Figure 2–1.)

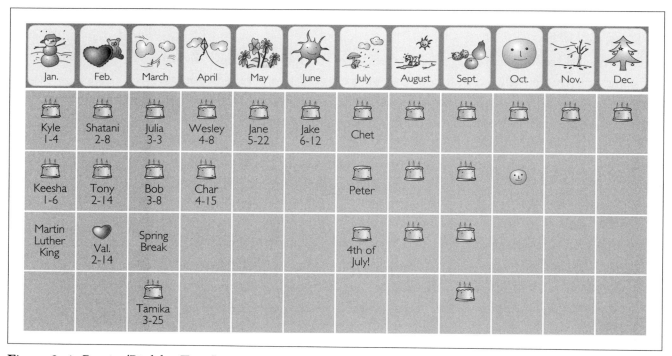

Figure 2–1 *Routine/Birthday Time Line*

Position the household flip calendar near the bulletin board calendar so it is accessible for student use and reference. This movable calendar makes it easy to mark special events, count days, and cross-reference the two calendar representations.

Developing Understandings About Weeks

1. Plan and schedule special weekly routines with your children. Use a class graph of favorite days of the week and decide upon the best day of the week for a special treat. (See Figure 2–2.) For example, every Monday children could do one of the following: bring a snack or small stuffed animal to keep them company while they work, play math board games, put puzzles together with friends, have a sing-along, do a special art project, use play dough, engage in free-choice activities, or help with a cooking project. Your particular group of children's interests and dispositions will influence the specific choices.

Favorite Day						
Sunday	**Monday**	**Tuesday**	**Wednesday**	**Thursday**	**Friday**	**Saturday**
Brian		Suki	Megan	Mitch	Kaitlin	Wes
		Beth	Geof	Alex	Claire	Joe
			Tamika		Chris	Ruby
			Jose		Kelly	Drew
			Emma		Gretchen	Bela
					Terry	Jake
					Brett	Shatari
						Char

Figure 2–2 *Favorite Day Graph*

Sunday	Monday	Tuesday	Wednesday	Thursday	Friday	Saturday
		Blue 1	Blue 2	Blue 3	Blue 4	Blue 5
Yellow 6	Yellow 7	Yellow 8	Yellow 9	Yellow 10	Yellow 11	Yellow 12
Purple 13	Purple 14	Purple 15	Purple 16	Purple 17	Purple 18	Purple 19
Orange 20	Orange 21	Orange 22	Orange 23	Orange 24	Orange 25	Orange 26
Green 27	Green 28	Green 29	Green 30			

Figure 2–3 *Repeating Pattern Calendar Display*

2. Calendars are rich in pattern opportunities. Frequently, bulletin boards feature repeating patterns within the calendar display. Rather than using an alternating color (a-b or a-b-c) pattern on the classroom calendar, consider calling attention to the idea of a week by using cutout numbers of one color for each week. For example, if you use umbrellas in April, make each horizontal calendar week a uniquely colored umbrella: Week 1—blue, Week 2—yellow, Week 3—purple, Week 4—orange, last row—green. (See Figure 2–3.) (**Note:** Ellison machines can generate these shapes easily enough to be replaced each year as the calendar specifics require.)

Developing Understandings About an Hour and Specific Time to the Minute

1. Use a large clock face that displays sixty-minute segments around the circumference of the circle. (See Figure 2–4; see also Blackline Masters.) Each day, count off and color one of the sixty segments depicted on the clock. During the daily calendar routine, use a marker to shade a single segment, representing one minute on the clock. Give students a copy of the sixty-minute clock so that they can fill in their own clocks as you demonstrate with the class model. Have them keep their clocks at their desks or taped into their math notebooks.

Help children notice the patterns of five changing colors each time you get to a bold *five* line segment. Each time you complete a cluster of five segments, discuss the number of minutes that have been colored in, and identify some things that could be accomplished in that amount of time. For example:

- In five minutes, we can get our lunches and get in line.
- In ten minutes, we can play four games of tic-tac-toe.
- In fifteen minutes, we can have a recess.

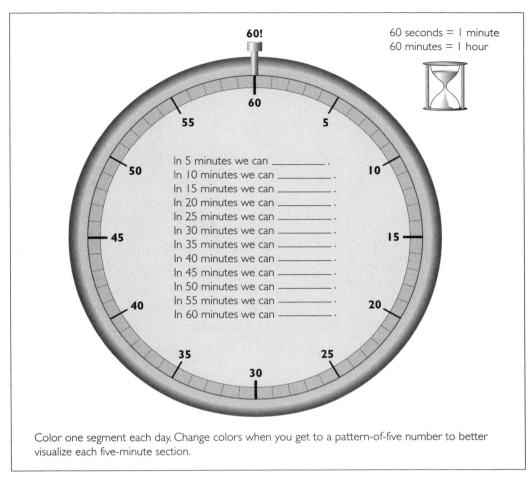

Figure 2–4 *Sixty-Second/Sixty-Minute Clock Display*

When you get all sixty segments filled in, have the class celebrate by inviting special guests to come for an hour or enjoy a special excursion or event.

2. Each day record the specific times of routinely scheduled events by listing them on the board or chart paper. Position small clocks with the accurate time representations next to the routine events listed for the day. (The clocks can be secured with adhesive magnets or tape.) (See Figure 2–5; see also Blackline Masters.) When it's time to transition from one activity to another, give a signal such as ringing a chime or flashing the light, and ask the class to take a look at the clock. Help the students get in the habit of looking at the details on the clock by calling their attention to

   • the distinction between the two hands
   • where the hands are in relation to the numbers on the clock
   • the differences between digital and analog representations

3. Use a timer to give the class a bit of extra time to visit with one another before the school day starts. Set the timer, write the amount of visiting time on the board, and give a signal when the time is up.

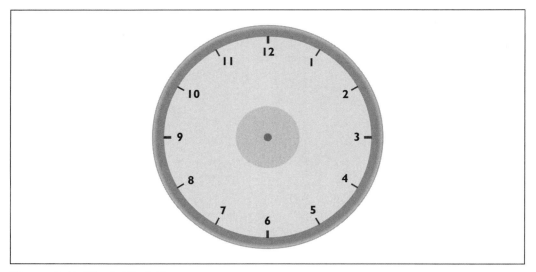

Figure 2–5 *Blank Clock Face*

4. Make a game of setting a timer as the children engage in various kinds of practice each day. For example, take one minute to see how many times the children can write their names, hop in place, or count.

5. Give students regular opportunities to see and manipulate a clock's hands (Judy clocks are ideal for this). Ask students to direct you to show specific times on the clock. As you demonstrate, remind children which is the minute hand and which is the hour hand. Gradually, have children lead the demonstrations.

 Night and Day Class Book

Overview

In this lesson, children focus on the familiar pattern of night and day. First they represent the night-and-day pattern with manipulative materials and then they illustrate the pattern for a class book.

Materials

◈ cubes, black and yellow, or 3-inch paper squares, black and yellow, enough for half of the class to have black and half to have yellow

◈ 12-by-18-inch construction paper, black and yellow, 1 sheet of each

◈ white crayon or marker

◈ black crayon or marker

◈ paper sack

◈ 9-by-12-inch construction paper, enough for half the class to have light colors and half to have dark colors

◈ crayons, enough for half the class to have light colors and half to have dark colors

Vocabulary: altogether, dark, day, double, earth, even, half, light, night, odd, opposite, pattern, predictable, total, twenty-four hours

Instructions

1. Prior to the lesson, prepare two lists, one for night and another for day, leaving room to add students' ideas. On the large black piece of construction paper, using the white crayon or marker, write a list like the following, about things that happen at night:

   • In the dark, dark night, we can see the moon and stars.
   • In the dark, dark night, fireworks go off on the Fourth of July.
   • In the dark, dark night, we turn on the lights.
   • In the dark, dark night, we go to sleep.
   • In the dark, dark night, owls are awake.

   On the large yellow piece of construction paper, using the black crayon or marker, make another list, this time of things that generally happen during the daytime. For example:

   • During the day, people often eat a midday meal that we call lunch.
   • During the day, when it's nice outside people can sunbathe.
   • During the day, bees and butterflies fly from flower to flower.
   • During the day, children go to school.

2. To begin the lesson, show the class the nighttime list you prepared. Ask students what else they think happens in the dark, dark night. Add their suggestions to the list.

3. Next, ask the children, "What is the opposite of night?" Have children help you spell as you fill in the blanks for the word *day* on the board. Explain that within each twenty-four-hour period, the earth spins around once, even though we can't feel it, and when we're facing away from the sun, we have nighttime. Daytime happens for the part of the earth that is facing toward the sun.

4. Show the class the daytime list you prepared. Again, have children add to the list.

5. Show the class the cubes (or paper squares) and explain that the yellow materials represent daytime and the black ones represent nighttime. Place all of the cubes (or paper squares) in the paper sack, give it a good shake, and ask each student to remove one cube.

6. Have all of the children with yellow cubes stand on one side of the room and the children with black cubes gather on the other side of the room. Count the two groups of cubes and compare them. Ask the children to think about questions like these:

   • Is one group larger than the other?
   • Are they equal? How do you know?

During the counting process, incorporate the concepts and language of *altogether*, *half*, *double*, and *total*.

7. Next, help the children arrange themselves in two parallel lines, creating a one-to-one correspondence between the two colors. Each person with a daytime cube will be across from a person with a nighttime cube. Use this arrangement to define the idea of even and odd numbers by checking to see whether or not each person has a partner. Discuss the language of *even* and *odd* and have the children help to demonstrate each. For example, children can count off one-two, three-four, five-six, and so on. If everyone has a partner, the final number is visibly even. If someone does not have a partner, *odd* is demonstrated by that unpaired person.

8. Create a lasting image of the night-and-day pattern by compiling a class book. Have the children with black cubes draw nighttime pictures on dark construction paper using light-colored crayons. Have the children with yellow cubes make daytime pictures on light-colored construction paper using dark-colored crayons. When everyone is finished, place the pages in a class book, alternating the night and day pictures to reinforce the pattern.

Extensions

❖ Have the class use watercolors to create crayon resist paintings of day and night. Have children draw pictures with crayons on white paper and then lightly brush them with watercolor paint in light blue for daytime or watered-down black for nighttime.

❖ As a class, make a Venn diagram of things that happen:
   • at night
   • during the day
   • during both night and day

 Clock Puzzles

Overview

In this lesson, students practice placing the numerals 1 through 12 on a clock puzzle. When the numbers have been accurately placed, the children use a moveable hour hand to practice the clockwise direction that shows passage of time by the hour. Learning about the function of the hour hand before thinking about the minute hand can help children understand what the hour hand actually measures.

Materials

❖ children's literature book with large analog clock illustrations, such as *Little Rabbit's First Time Book*, by Alan Baker (1999) or *Tell Time at the Farm*, by Stephanie Ryder (1996)

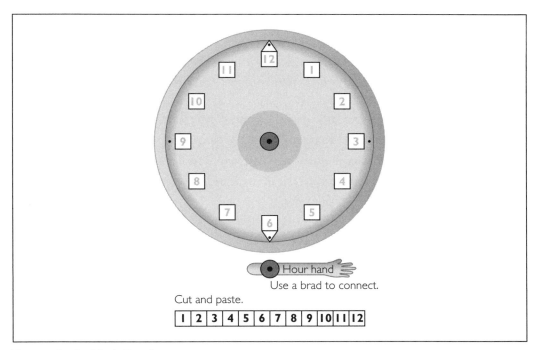

Figure 2–6 *Clock Puzzle*

❧ large Judy clock
❧ clock puzzle, 1 per student (see Figure 2–6; see also Blackline Masters)
❧ numerals 1 through 12, 1 set per student (see Blackline Masters)
❧ metal brads, 1 per student
❧ analog clock
❧ digital clock
❧ optional: chart paper

Vocabulary: analog clock, around, bottom, clock face, clockwise, counting numbers, digital clock, hands of a clock, historical, hours, long, minutes, past, short, telling time, top, 1, 2, 3, 4, 5, 6, 7, 8, 9, 10, 11, 12

Instructions

1. After reading a story about clocks and telling time, close the book and ask the children to describe a clock. Ask students to retell important ideas from the book. On the board or chart paper, list what the children say, such as

   • The long hand shows the number of minutes in an hour.
   • The short hand helps people know the hour.
   • Twelve is the number at the top of the clock.

   Use the large Judy clock to demonstrate the ideas. Count the numbers around the clock. Help the children make sense of peculiar terms like *clock face* and *the hands on a clock* by discussing and defining those words.

2. Ask the children to describe the kinds of clocks that they have at home. Show them an analog clock and a digital clock. Discuss similarities and differences between analog clocks and digital clocks. Talk with the class about the most common times of the day that family members are likely to use or check their clocks.

3. Explain that when people first began to use clocks hundreds of years ago, most clocks showed only the hour hand and that people were able to do a pretty good job of telling time by looking at just the hour hand. With the Judy clock, keep the minute hand covered, and rotate the hour hand in a clockwise direction as you discuss approximate time to the hour.

4. Show the children the clock puzzle. Discuss and/or model cutting the numbers apart, matching them to the correct positions on the puzzle, and gluing them down. Distribute the materials. As the children work, walk around the classroom and help them connect the cutout hour hands to the clock faces with metal brads.

5. When the puzzles are complete, have the class practice showing time to the hour. Have the children practice clockwise movement by showing the time from one hour to the next. Have them take turns suggesting hours for the class to show on the clocks.

6. Discuss the fact that the hour hand moves quite slowly, so that it's hard to see the movement on a regular clock. Have the class demonstrate the position of the hour hand when it is halfway past an hour. Throughout the school year, at the beginning of math class, use the clocks to give children quick repeated practice with the hour hand.

Extensions

◈ Have the children write the symbolic representation for various hours so that they become comfortable with this convention. For example, tell them to show 12:00 on their clocks and to write the time in their math notebooks, show 3:00 and write the time, and so on.

◈ Ask children to draw a copy of their clocks in their math notebooks. Draw a circle and demonstrate writing the *12, 3, 6,* and *9* to help with placement of the other numerals.

 Week Stomp

Overview

In this lesson, children practice the days-of-the-week sequence. When they are shown word cards, printed with the names of the weekdays and the corresponding number of symbols, children chant the word and stomp the appropriate number of times. Seeing the visual, feeling the movement, and chanting the words help students commit the language and sequence to memory.

Materials

◈ large calendar

◈ 4-by-6-inch index cards, 7

◈ optional: chart paper

Vocabulary: calendar, fifth, first, fourth, Friday, Monday, order, pattern, repeating, Saturday, second, seventh, sixth, Sunday, third, Thursday, Tuesday, Wednesday, week, weekday, weekend

Instructions

1. Before class, prepare the weekday word cards. On each index card, print a day of the week and a symbol to indicate the ordinal number of the day, as illustrated.

| Sunday | Monday | Tuesday | Wednesday | Thursday | Friday | Saturday |
| * | ** | *** | **** | ***** | ****** | ******* |

2. Begin by showing the class the stack of the seven weekday word cards. Reveal the Sunday card, explaining that it is the first day of the week on calendars. Read the word and ask what day of the week is likely to come next. Discuss the fact that the days of the week are always in the same order. Call attention to the large calendar and reinforce the weekday sequence.

3. Show each card in order. Tell the class that the symbol on the card shows where that day happens in the week. Explain that Sunday is the first day, so it gets one symbol; Monday is the second day, so it gets two symbols. Have the class look at the Sunday word card, chant "Sunday" and stomp once; look at the Monday card, chant "Monday" and stomp twice; look at the Tuesday card, chant "Tuesday," and stomp three times; and so on, through Saturday.

Sunday * stomp

Monday ** stomp, stomp

Tuesday *** stomp, stomp, stomp

Wednesday **** stomp, stomp, stomp, stomp

Thursday ***** stomp, stomp, stomp, stomp, stomp

Friday ****** stomp, stomp, stomp, stomp, stomp, stomp

Saturday ******* stomp, stomp, stomp, stomp, stomp, stomp, stomp

4. The chanting of the seven days can be done quickly and repeated over an extended period of time. Add a special movement to indicate each day of the week.

For example, when students say "Wednesday" and stomp four times, they can also wave their hands in the air.

5. Once the children are familiar with the routine, you can write the weekday sequence and dots (or symbols) on chart paper or the board and invite a student to lead the class through the activity.

6. Ask questions about ordinal numbers relating to the days of the week, such as these:
   - Which is the first day of the week? The second? The third?
   - Which day is the last day of the week?
   - What days do we call the *weekend*?

Extension
❧ After giving each day of the week its own motion, make the game more challenging by having students commit the seven-day sequence of motions to memory.

 Favorite Days

Overview
In this lesson, students consider their own weekly routines and decide upon a day of the week that is their personal favorite. Eve Bunting's book *The Wednesday Surprise* serves as a springboard for this activity. It's a story of family kindness, perseverance, and anticipation. Readers quickly realize that Wednesday is the best day of the week for the family in this book. After processing the story, the class creates a graph about favorite weekdays.

Materials
❧ *The Wednesday Surprise*, by Eve Bunting (1989)
❧ commercial cutouts such as suns or stars, large enough to write a child's name on them, 2 per child (**Note:** Many school picture companies provide teachers with individual small adhesive photos of their students. These photographs can be substituted for the commercial cutouts. An Ellison machine can also be used to create the cutouts.)
❧ chart paper, 2 or 3 sheets
❧ classroom calendar

Vocabulary: Friday, Monday, predictable, routine, Saturday, Sunday, Thursday, Tuesday, Wednesday, week, weekdays

Instructions

1. Prior to the lesson, prepare a "Favorite Days of the Week" graph on chart paper. (See Figure 2–7.)

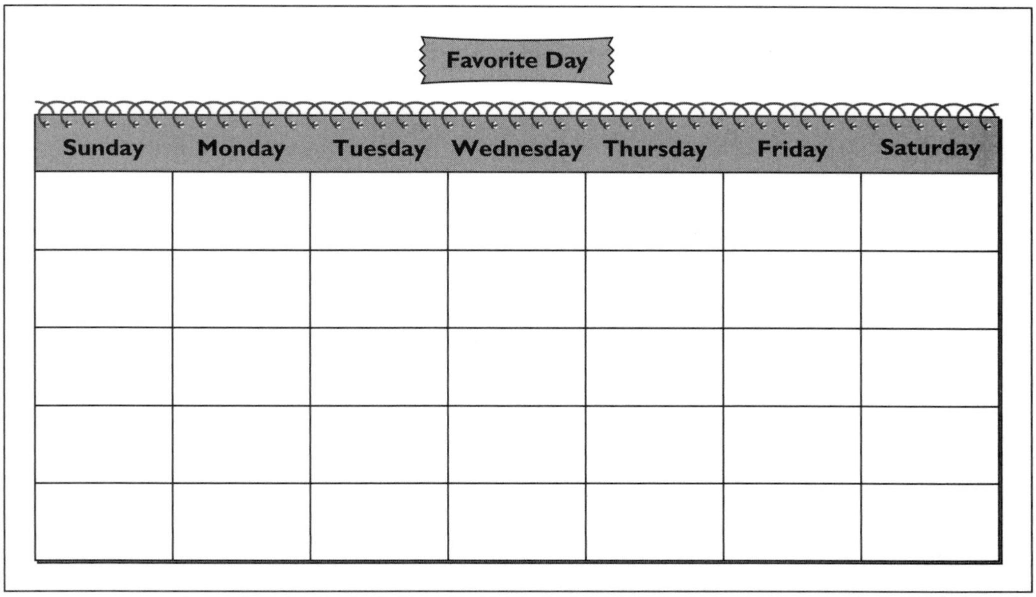

Figure 2–7 *Blank Favorite Day Graph*

2. Begin the lesson by reading *The Wednesday Surprise* to the class. Discuss the reasons that Wednesdays were so important to Anna and her grandmother. Ask the children to think of words that describe how Anna's family must have felt when they realized how Anna and her grandmother had been spending their Wednesday evenings.

3. Ask children to think about their own weekly schedules and what their favorite day is. As children consider possibilities, review the weekdays on the class calendar. Brainstorm things that happen in a week and share a few reasons that a particular day might be special. If needed, provide the children with some examples, such as the following:

   • A child I knew liked Friday nights best because Friday was "pizza and a movie night" at her house.
   • Another child liked Wednesdays because he always went to a friend's house after school.
   • A third child liked Thursday because his dad picked him up from the after-school program.

4. Have partners talk to one other about some of their favorite events in a week. Set a specific amount of time for students to decide upon a favorite day. Be prepared to assist some children by discussing special activities within the weekly schedule at school.

5. Distribute blank 8½-by-11-inch paper and ask each student to write (or draw) about his or her favorite day. When everyone is done, collect the papers and sequence them in order from Sunday to Saturday to create a *Favorite Days* class book.

Figure 2–8 *Favorite Day Graph*

6. As the children work on their pages, walk around the classroom and give each child a calendar cutout for the class graph that you prepared ahead of time. Have the children write their names on the cutouts and place them on the graph under their favorite day of the week. (See Figure 2–8.)

7. When everyone has contributed to the graph, ask the children what the graph is about. Discuss what they notice about the results. Record true math statements on chart paper. Here are some examples:

• Eight people chose Saturday as their favorite day; both Tuesday and Thursday were chosen by two people.

• Twenty-five people have their names on the graph.

• Eight was the most number of people on a day.

• Nobody picked Monday, so that is zero, or the least favorite day.

Draw attention to amount comparisons and assist the children with mathematical vocabulary. Post the true math statements next to the graph.

Extensions

❖ Ask the children to help you identify the day of the week that was selected least frequently. Emphasize the language of *less*, *fewer*, and *least*. If the identified day is a school day, for example, Monday, plan a special event to incorporate into your weekly routine, such as bringing a snack from home or playing a favorite class game.

❖ Have students make predictions about how another class's graph might look. Invite another class to complete the activity, and then compare the information.

 ## Monthly Wonder Walks

Overview

This lesson establishes a monthly routine—taking a class walk—that directs children's attention toward visual patterns of change in the outdoor environment. Before the walk begins, children take time to wonder about the changes they might see. After returning to the classroom, students contribute to a class book by recording what they've noticed. Wonder walks provide an opportunity for students to learn about the months within a calendar year through observation and inquiry.

Materials

❖ chart paper, at least 2 sheets
❖ crayons, enough for the class to share
❖ 9-by-12-inch construction paper, 2 pieces
❖ optional: magnifying glasses and/or cameras, 1 per student
❖ optional: clipboards, 1 per student

Vocabulary: April, August, December, environment, February, January, July, June, March, May, months, notice, November, observe, October, record, September, wonder

Instructions

1. Around the first of each month, take the class on a walk around the school grounds and look for details in the environment. Before you take the first walk, explain to the children that each month, the group will take a walk using the same route every time. Tell them that they will first make predictions about what they might see, and once outside, they will look for special details, find things to wonder about, and look for things that are wonderful and special. Explain that small details might be nests in trees, the shapes that clouds are making, shiny

stones, or iridescent wings on beetles. Discuss the places that children might look for interesting things, such as in the air, on the building, on the ground, up in the sky, or on plants and trees. Let them know they will record what they find for a monthly *Wonder Walk* class book.

2. Introduce and define *environment* as the area that surrounds us, and explain that there are many things in our environment to wonder about. Tell the class, for example, some children have wondered the following:

   • What is our building made of?
   • What's blooming right now?
   • Are there any flowers blooming this month? What color are they?
   • Are there clouds in the sky today? What do they look like?
   • Will we see any birds or planes? Can we hear them?
   • How many people rode bikes to school today? How many wheels are there altogether?
   • Who cleans up the trash around our school? Should we help?

   After offering a few examples to get things started, ask the children to think of things that they plan to pay special attention to. Record on chart paper some of the ideas using the sentence starter "I wonder . . ."

3. As you get ready for the first walk, emphasize the observational focus of the excursion. Give the children clipboards and pencils to encourage on-the-spot recording, if appropriate. Magnifying glasses and/or cameras are also useful tools to help the children focus on specifics and details. During the walk, stop every now and then and ask children to take a mental snapshot of something that they may wish to draw on their *Wonder Walk* page for the class book.

4. It is useful (and fun) to set up an auditory signal that will let everyone know when something special has been found. For example, one class may choose clapping, whereas another group may decide a quacking sound will best get everyone's attention.

5. When you and the class have returned to the classroom, play some quiet music and give students a little relaxation time to decide what they want to draw and write about.

6. Pass out blank sheets of 8½-by-11-inch paper. Because they tend to include more detail in their recordings if they begin with pencil, tell children to create their initial drawings with pencil only. Let them know that they will color them later. To the degree that it is reasonable, have children write about their experiences. To increase children's writing confidence and help them get their ideas on paper, record the correct spelling of requested words on the chalkboard.

7. After each class member has contributed a page, and the monthly book is complete, make a cover with the two sheets of construction paper. Use student drawings, photos, or magazine pictures to decorate it. Prominently display the name of the month on the cover so that children can easily recognize the month. Students will enjoy rereading and comparing these books as the year progresses. The previous months' *Wonder Walk* books can be used as a reference when the class prepares to look for changes in the new month.

Extension

❖ At the end of the year, have parent volunteers help rearrange the pages to create a *Wonder Walk* yearbook for each individual student in the class.

 ## My Year Book

Overview

In this lesson, students create personal monthly year books after becoming familiar with Maurice Sendak's *Chicken Soup with Rice: A Book of Months*.

Materials

❖ *Chicken Soup with Rice*, by Maurice Sendak (1962)
❖ pad of 18-by-24-inch chart paper, lined
❖ clip art for each season of the year, enough for the class
❖ 9-by-12-inch construction paper, 1 sheet per pair of students
❖ twelve-month spiral calendar

Vocabulary: April, August, calendar, December, February, January, July, June, March, May, month, November, October, September, year

Instructions

1. Before class, prepare a *Chicken Soup with Rice* text chart. Use one page of the chart paper pad for each month. On each page, write the month and copy the appropriate text from the book.

2. Prepare a sample of the year book that students will make. To do this, fold each of three sheets of blank 8½-by-11-inch paper vertically and horizontally. Label each minipage with a month. Create a border design by using clip art that provides a seasonal cue for the month. Cut each sheet into four small pages. Use half a sheet of construction paper to make front and back covers. Sequence the pages by month, beginning with the month in which you start school. Staple them together with the covers. Prepare a book for each student. (**Note:** Parents and volunteers are often willing to help make the books and create the monthly designs.)

3. Begin the lesson by reading the book *Chicken Soup with Rice*. As you turn the pages from one month to the next, ask the children who have a birthday in that month to raise their hands. (Some children may not know the name of the month that they were born, so it's helpful to have that information handy.)

4. Explain to the children that there are twelve months in every year and they always happen in the same order. Show the monthly sequence with the spiral flip calendar to reinforce and demonstrate this sequence.

5. At the beginning of each month, display the appropriate *Chicken Soup with Rice* text chart. During opening routines, include the month's verse. Encourage the children to join in with the reading as you point to the words.

6. When the children are familiar with the *Chicken Soup with Rice* book, explain that everyone in the class will make his or her own personal year book. Pass out the little books to the children. Show them the sample year book that you have prepared, and read the names of the months on each page as they follow along in their own books.

7. Begin with the month that you start school and invite the children to illustrate the page with something special about that month. Some classes choose to draw monthly self-portraits; others draw seasonal pictures. (See Figure 2–9.) When everyone is done, collect the books and store them until the next month. Each month, help the children make sure that they are on the right page by reviewing the sequence of the months.

8. At the end of the school year, send the books home so children can complete them over the summer months.

Extension
◈ Play the musical version of *Chicken Soup with Rice* (King 2004) as part of your weekly calendar routine.

Four-Season Collage

Overview
In this lesson children sort a variety of magazine, catalog, and calendar pictures in order to practice identifying seasonal changes. Once the pictures are sorted, they create collages for each of the four seasons. The artwork is displayed and referenced throughout the year.

Figure 2–9 *A child's illustration for her own personal year book.*

Materials

◈ a book about seasonal changes such as *A Busy Year*, by Leo Lionni (1992); *Frederick*, by Leo Lionni (1967); *The Seasons of Arnold's Apple Tree*, by Gail Gibbons (1984); *The Reasons for Seasons*, by Gail Gibbons (1995); or *A Field of Sunflowers*, by Neil Johnson (1997)

◈ magazines, catalogs, and calendars with pictures that show different seasons, at least 40 to 100 pictures

- 4-by-6-inch index cards, unlined, 16
- light-colored poster board, 4 pieces
- zip-top bags, 4

Vocabulary: April, August, autumn, December, fall, February, January, July, June, March, May, month, November, October, seasons, September, spring, summer, winter, year

Instructions

1. Before class, prepare four sets of seasonal word cards. On a blank index card, write *fall*. On the next, write *winter*. On the third, write *spring,* and on the fourth, *summer*. Repeat three more times.

   Also, prepare four sets of seasonal pictures for students to sort during the lesson. Cut out pictures from your collection of magazines, catalogs, and calendars that can be identified as fall, winter, spring, or summer. Each set should contain at least ten pictures. Put each collection in a zip-top bag.

2. Introduce this lesson by reading one of the suggested children's literature books to reinforce seasonal understandings and develop vocabulary. After reading the book, review the names of the four seasons with the class. Show and identify the written words for each of the four seasons.

3. Position the word cards so all children can see them and play a game called *Guess the Season*. To start the game, describe some attributes of one of the four seasons and ask the children to point to the appropriate word card. For example, tell the children to point to the name of the season that is very cold in many places. Explain that this season often has ice and snow. Continue seasonal descriptions until you feel that the class is comfortable with the basic distinctions between the four seasons. Besides providing a way to check for understanding, this game also gives you and the children a chance to identify and discuss seasonal changes in your particular location.

4. Now, show children a bag containing a collection of seasonal pictures. Without looking, pull out a picture. Show it to the class and ask which season the students think the picture best represents. Place the picture near the corresponding word card. Repeat this process a few times.

5. Organize the children into four groups around the room. Give each group a set of the seasonal word cards and a set of pictures. Explain to the children that they will sort the pictures as you just did. Each person will take a turn selecting a picture and placing it with the appropriate word card.

6. When the sorting has been completed, reorganize the pictures into four large collections, one for each season. Redistribute the pictures so that each group has

pictures of only one season. Tell the class that each group will use the pictures to make a collage of a particular season.

7. Model the procedure of using glue to attach pictures to a large piece of poster board. Ask students to think about how they will divide the pictures and cooperate to glue them onto the poster board to create a seasonal collage. After they share their ideas, hand out the materials (glue and posterboard).

8. Collect the posters and give them plenty of time to dry.

9. Display the collage posters, labeled with the names of the seasons.

Extensions

❖ Include the names of the appropriate months on the seasonal posters.
❖ Choose a flowering tree in your school area and do the following:

  • Have the children create seasonal drawings of changes that occur in the tree during the yearly cycle.
  • Periodically take class photos within view of the tree to note seasonal changes.
  • Create seasonal information posters that include photos and nonfiction information about the tree.

Durations of Time

Overview

In this lesson students compare durations of time as they become familiar with a variety of timers. Exploring a variety of timers gives children an opportunity to think about different lengths of time and what can be accomplished in a given duration of time.

Materials

A collection of timers, such as

❖ cooking timers, 2
❖ sand timers, 2
❖ stopwatches, 2
❖ wristwatches, 5
❖ plastic wands filled with glitter and oil, 2
❖ analog clock, 1
❖ digital clock, 1

Note: Ask parents to help with gathering together items for this collection. In a letter, let parents know that their children will be studying concepts of time and include your wish list of timing devices and a request for their help. Encourage families to discuss their clocks, watches, and other timers with their children.

Vocabulary: analog, clock, digital, glitter wand, length (of time), less, longer, minutes, more, seconds, shorter, timer, watch

Instructions

1. Have the children sit in a large circle. Show them the various timers. As you introduce each timer, describe its typical use, give information about how the timer works, and pass it around so that the children get a chance to closely investigate it. Caution the class about any timers that may be fragile. On the board, make a list of the timers in your collection as a way to help children remember the various names of the devices and also to keep track of them.

2. Put the timing devices such as the clocks, watches, and kitchen timers on a display table or shelf so that the children can see and handle them over time. If you are concerned about small items, such as the watches, getting damaged or lost, place them on a tray and make them available during supervised times.

3. After the children have had a chance to look at the timers, pick two of them, such as the glitter wand and the sand timer, and ask children to predict which one will take the longest amount of time to shift its contents from one end to another. Ask partners to talk to one another about which timer will take longer and how they might test the timers to check their predictions. Have children share their choices and reasoning. For instance, a child might say, "I think the wand will take longer because it is longer than the sand timer," or "The glitter in the wand is bigger, so the glitter will go down faster."

4. Have the class share ideas about how to test the timers. Some children may suggest that you start the timers at the same time and make a direct comparison, while others may suggest using the clock to "time the timers."

5. Have the class complete a repetitive task for the duration of each timer. For instance, using the glitter wand, ask the students to write their names or connect cubes or make tally marks until the timer runs out. Repeat this process using a second timer. Then ask the children if they can tell from their results which of the timers took longer and have them explain their reasoning.

6. Give children many repeated opportunities to gauge durations of time. Choose repetitive activities that can be done quickly as a warm-up to math class or as a way to transition from one activity to another. Set a timer or directly compare timers.

Extension
◈ Make lists of things that can be accomplished in the time it takes for various timers to get to their stopping points.

Time Stories

Overview

In this lesson children review the ideas that they have learned about various aspects of time. They play the game *Guess My Rule* and then incorporate concepts of time into their own personal stories.

Materials

- math notebooks or index cards, 1 per student
- paper that your class likes such as 8½-by-11-inch colored or bordered, at least 2 sheets per student
- books about time such as *The Grouchy Ladybug*, by Eric Carle (1996), *Pigs on a Blanket*, by Amy Axelrod (1998), *Clocks and How They Go*, by Gail Gibbons (1979), and *10 Minutes till Bedtime*, by Peggy Rathmann (1998)
- crayons and markers, enough for the class to share
- sticky notes, 3 per student

Vocabulary: afternoon, April, August, counting numbers (1, 2, 3 . . .), day, December, evening, fall, February, fiction, Friday, hour, January, July, June, March, May, midnight, minute, Monday, morning, night, nonfiction, November, October, Saturday, September, spring, Sunday, summer, Thursday, Tuesday, Wednesday, winter

Instructions

1. Introduce this lesson by playing a game of *Guess My Rule* to help children think about various aspects of time. Draw a large circle on the board. Generate some words and symbols that convey ideas about time and put them inside the circle. Invite the students to do the same. Some time ideas that could go in the circle include

   - time notations to the hour and minute, such as 11:30
   - lengths of time, such as a half hour and five minutes
   - Time-of-day words, such as *morning, afternoon, evening, midnight*
   - days of the week
   - months of the year
   - seasons

   Now ask for some nonexamples—words that do not relate to time, such as colors, foods, school supplies, and names of objects. Place these outside of the circle.

2. Read the list of topics that has been created within the circle to call attention to the concepts of time. Ask if anyone can state the rule. Explain to the children that they will be creating individual stories that must include three ideas about time. Tell them that the list can help them get started.

3. Let the children know that they can write about things that really happen in life (nonfiction) or about pretend, made-up ideas (fiction). It can be helpful to provide time for children to look over familiar stories that include concepts of time. Consider reading a nonfiction story such as *Clocks and How They Go* or the fictional story of one little boy's fantastic bedtime countdown, 10 *Minutes till Bedtime*.

4. Ask questions to help students think about whether their stories will be fiction or nonfiction, funny or serious, and so on.

5. In their math notebooks or on index cards, have the children make notes and/or drawings to indicate ideas that they might include in their stories. Some children may benefit from sentence starters such as these:
   - The clock struck midnight and . . .
   - There were _____ minutes left in the game and . . .
   - The cookies had been in the oven for _____ minutes when . . .
   - Last year I . . .
   - On Saturday . . .
   - The little girl was 7 and her grandmother was _____. They liked to . . .

6. When you think the students are ready, have them write and illustrate their stories. Provide the class with materials that are familiar and comfortable for them, such as the paper they prefer and crayons and markers for illustrations. Support children during the writing process and assist with needed words and symbols.

7. When the stories are almost done, give each child three small sticky notes. Ask them to place a note next to each idea that relates to time as a self-assessment for the completion of the assignment.

8. During a whole-class discussion, make a list of types of time ideas students used in their stories such as months, weeks, telling time, and so on. Indicate the frequency of each type of time idea by putting a check mark next to it each time it is used in the stories. For example, consider *birthdays* as a time idea. Initially record the word and then place a check mark next to it each time a class member refers to a birthday.

Extension

❖ Using ideas that pertain to time, make up stories that include familiar characters. For example, have the class help you include a season, an age, and a time of day for a story about *Little Bear* (Minarik 1957) or a Magic Tree House (Osborne 2001) story.

Area

CHAPTER 3

Introduction

Children have a natural tendency to think of measurement as the one-dimensional attribute of length. The topic of area extends children's thinking into two dimensions. Area is about covering surfaces. Children have some awareness of surface area from their own blankets and quilts and experience with flooring patterns, hopscotch games, and sidewalk lines. Area has powerful connections to geometry.

The lessons in this chapter give students opportunities to compare and order surface areas and develop vocabulary. Children consider shapes and part-whole relationships as well as the number of units that is required to fill a space. Several of the lessons offer opportunities to record results, and all of the lessons require students to predict, estimate, and communicate with others.

Square Puzzles

Overview
In this lesson children create a puzzle from a 10-by-10-square piece of grid paper. They divide the square into four or five sections, cut them out, and then find and compare the areas of the resulting pieces.

Materials
◈ half-inch grid paper, 10-by-10 squares, 1 per student (see Blackline Masters)
◈ half-inch grid overhead transparency, 10 by 10

Vocabulary: area, big, bigger, biggest, equal, fewer, grid, least, less, more, most, pieces, rectangle, same number, small, smaller, smallest, square

Instructions

1. Show the children a 10-by-10 half-inch paper grid. Discuss the small squares within the larger shape and explain that this arrangement is called a *grid*. Ask the

children to tell what they know about squares. This conversation should include ideas like the following:

- Squares have four sides and four corners or angles.
- Squares are special kinds of rectangles with sides that are all the same length.
- Squares have special corners called right angles.

Discuss and count the number of small squares in the grid. Explain to the students that they will use a square grid like the one you are showing them, which contains one hundred small squares, to make a puzzle.

2. Create a sample puzzle using the overhead transparency grid. Using a marker, outline a section of the grid, staying on the lines, and then cut that section out. The section can be any size and shape. Outline another section, and again cut it out. Repeat until you have three or four puzzle pieces and have used the entire 10-by-10 grid. Describe your actions as you draw each outline and carefully cut on the lines. You may wish to color each piece with a different-colored marker so that the pieces can still be easily seen when they are repositioned into the original square.

3. When you are done, compare the areas of the pieces. Discuss their relative sizes by asking the children questions such as

- Which piece is the smallest? How do you know?
- Which is the largest? How do you know?
- Are there any that are the same size? How do you know?
- Are there any that are the same shape? How can you tell?

4. Elicit from the children the various methods of counting they used and how they kept track of the square units already counted. Although it is natural for children to count by ones, some arrangements lend themselves to counting by twos or threes, or to counting the outside perimeter of the shape and then the interior.

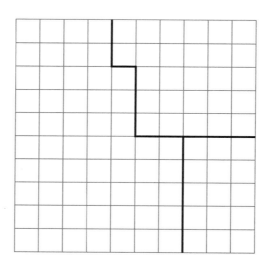

5. Have the children help describe how the pieces should be positioned to make the original square. Discuss matching lines by looking at connecting corners or angles.

6. Give each child his or her own 10-by-10-square grid. Set a limit for the number of puzzle pieces that they should create, such as four or five. Ask one or more class members to restate the directions for this activity in their own words before children begin to work. Post simple directions and your sample puzzle to help students remember the steps.

7. If appropriate, have each child record the following information about his or her completed puzzle.
   - How many pieces does your puzzle have?
   - What is the number of square units in each of your puzzle pieces?
   - What is the number of square units in your puzzle when you arrange the pieces into the original grid shape?

8. Have students pair up to solve one another's puzzles. Seeing the 10-by-10 squares in different configurations helps them see that, though a shape changes, its area stays the same (conservation of area).

Extensions
◈ Instead of giving students 10-by-10-square grids, use different-sized rectangles.
◈ Have students make puzzles using squares from non-grid paper. Discuss ways that the areas of the pieces could be compared.
◈ Use a 1–100 chart and discuss with students the possible vertical and diagonal patterns of the numbers in the chart.

 Pattern Block Designs

Overview
In this lesson, students use pattern blocks to find different ways to cover three hexagons. By making substitutions, such as two green triangles for one blue rhombus, students discover that different units can cover the same amount of space, or area.

Materials
◈ pattern blocks, enough so that each pair of students has access to at least 2 yellow hexagons, 4 red trapezoids, 6 blue rhombi, 6 tan parallelograms, 4 blue squares, and 12 green triangles
◈ optional: chart paper

Vocabulary: area, blue rhombus, design, green triangle, inside, orange square, red trapezoid, shape, space, substitute, tan parallelogram, yellow hexagon

Instructions

1. Before beginning the lesson, give students repeated opportunities to explore the pattern blocks so that they become familiar with the relationships between the pieces. Have students discuss the geometric and color names for the pattern blocks and compare the sizes of the different shapes. As children make comparisons, have them count the sides and corners or angles of each type of block.

2. Distribute pattern blocks to each pair of students. Tell them to locate a yellow hexagon. Ask them to create the same shape by placing different pattern blocks on top of the yellow one so it is completely covered. When everyone is ready, ask the following:

   • Are the yellow hexagon and the one you created from the other blocks the same shape? How do you know?
   • Are there gaps or overlaps?
   • Does the new configuration cover the same amount of area as the original hexagon?

      Have volunteers describe how they covered the yellow hexagon. Record the different ways on the board or chart paper.

3. Next, ask children to think about making substitutions for three hexagons instead of one. Ask: What kind of pieces could be used? How many do you think would be needed?

4. Now have the children work with their partners to find and record as many solutions as possible to this problem. Explain that when everyone is ready, the class will discuss the different ways the problem can be solved.

5. Observe the children as they work, and informally discuss different solution possibilities. For instance, a child may have used two red trapezoids and later substituted three green triangles for one of the trapezoids.

6. When everyone is ready, lead a whole-class discussion. Have several children share their findings. Record student thinking and display it in the room with examples of each pattern block piece. Discuss which type of pattern block covers the most area. Talk about which shapes cover more than half of a hexagon, exactly half, or less than half. Reinforce the language *same area*.

Extensions

◈ Focus on multiples. Have students cover three hexagons with one particular type of shape. For example, using two trapezoids to cover each hexagon provides a context for counting by twos. Using blue rhombi encourages counting by threes; using green triangles encourages counting by sixes.

◈ Have students make a design with pattern blocks and then create a congruent shape by making substitutions.

 Yarn Loops

Overview

Pairs of students create "yarn loop" shapes, which they fill with materials such as tiles, cubes, and lima beans. Children then count the number of units they used, share their results, and consider why the areas of their yarn loops are not the same.

Materials

◈ jump rope or very large piece of yarn

◈ yarn, 6 to 12 inches long, 1 per pair of students

◈ variety of tiles, cubes, lima beans, or other materials for filling the yarn loops

◈ clear or masking tape

◈ *Yarn Loops* recording sheets, 1 per pair of students (see Blackline Masters)

◈ paper of one size, enough sheets to fill the large yarn loop

◈ optional: chart paper

Vocabulary: area, count, inside, interior, length, loop, measure, shape, yarn

Instructions

1. Introduce this activity on a large scale by positioning a jump rope or very large piece of yarn into a big circular loop or shape of your choice. Ask the children to think about some things that might fit inside the loop. Looking around the classroom, children might suggest objects such as chairs, books, or pieces of construction paper. Next speculate about things that wouldn't fit in the loop because they are too large.

2. Use consistently sized paper that is available in the room and ask the children to estimate how many sheets of this paper will fit in the interior of the loop; then fill the shape and keep track of the count.

3. On a large piece of chart paper or the board, record

   • the students' predictions
   • the number of units counted

   Discuss the results.

4. Explain that, like you did, partners will arrange a yarn loop into a shape they like, tape it in place, and then measure its area by filling the loop with a material of their

choice. Instruct them to predict the area before they begin to fill the shape. Remind the children not to leave spaces between the units or to change the position of their yarn loop once it's set. Explain that when the area has been filled, they are to count and record the number of units that were needed to cover the area inside of the yarn loop on their recording sheet. Show the class the small pieces of yarn (preferably all the same length) and the variety of measurement materials they can choose from.

5. When the recordings have been completed, have the class discuss the results. On the board or a large piece of chart paper, display the range of numbers that were recorded and ask children to consider the reasons that different numbers were counted. Discuss the size of the objects used to fill the loops as well as the positioning of the yarn loops.

Extensions

❧ Continue to experiment with positioning large items inside a large jump-rope circle. Use the same unit at any given time. For instance, see how many children can fit inside the yarn loop in standing positions, sitting positions, and so on. Take pictures to compare the visual representations.

❧ Have children trade yarn loops and materials, then reposition them to see if the area changes.

 ## Cookie Cutters

Overview

In this lesson, children, working in pairs, use homemade play dough and a variety of cookie cutters to make "cookies." They then compare the shapes and areas of their cookies.

Materials

❧ cookie cutters of various sizes and shapes, 1 per student
❧ play dough, 1 handful per student (see Instruction 1)
❧ lima beans, about 50
❧ small plastic bags, 1 per student
❧ overhead transparencies, 1 or 2

Vocabulary: area, big, bigger, biggest, compare, flat, large, larger, largest, same size, size, small, smaller, smallest, space

Instructions

1. Prior to the lesson, prepare the play dough using one of the following recipes.

No-Cook Play Dough

3 cups flour
3 cups salt
3 tablespoons alum

Combine ingredients and slowly add water a little at a time. Mix well with a spoon. As mixture thickens, continue mixing with your hands until it has the feel of clay. If it feels too dry, add more water. If it's too sticky, add equal parts flour and salt. Yield: about thirty walnut-sized pieces.

Traditional Play Dough

1 cup flour
1 cup warm water
2 teaspoons cream of tartar
1 teaspoon oil
$\frac{1}{4}$ *cup salt*
food coloring

Mix all ingredients, adding food coloring last. Stir over medium heat until smooth. Remove from pan and knead until blended smooth. Cool. Place in plastic bag or airtight container. (**Note:** This play dough will last for a long time. Yield: about ten to fifteen walnut-sized pieces.)

Place a handful of dough in each small plastic bag.

2. Begin the lesson by showing the class the play dough you've prepared. Model the process of flattening a handful of play dough like a pancake. Press a cookie cutter into the dough and peel away the extra scraps. Repeat the process using a second cookie cutter and ask the children which cookie seems to take up more space, or area. Have a couple of students examine the cookies to decide which one is the biggest, that is, has the most area.

3. Explain to the children that each of them will have a chance to make a play dough cookie and then compare it with a partner's play dough cookie. Give each child a small handful of play dough and a cookie cutter. Tell partners that once they make cookies, they are to compare them and decide which is larger. (Be sure that partners have different-shaped cookie cutters.) Give each pair a sheet of paper and ask the children to record their comparisons like this: "We think _____ 's cookie covers more space than _____ 's cookie". Have students indicate the cookie cutters that they used by writing their shapes, such as star or clown, or by tracing around the shapes with a pencil.

4. If possible, have children exchange cookie cutters and repeat the process. This allows them to investigate a variety of shapes.

5. When the students have had a chance to create and compare their cookies, have a whole-class discussion about which cookie cutters make cookies with the greatest area and which make cookies with the least area. Ask if there are any cookie cutters that make cookies almost the same size.

6. Investigate the area of the cookies in another way. Use an overhead projector. Position a couple of cookie cutters side by side on a blank transparency. Trace the shapes and then remove the cookie cutters. Place a single layer of lima beans as close together as possible inside each outline. Ask the class to help you count the beans that cover the interior of each of the shapes. Compare the differences between the amounts. Ask, "Are the shapes as similar as they appeared to be when the play dough cookies were compared?" Discuss the idea that sometimes visual cues can be surprising, for example, long shapes can look bigger, but they may not have as much area inside.

Extensions
❖ Have the children use jar lids instead of cookie cutters and make circles using play dough. They can compare the circles using both direct comparison and lima beans.
❖ Have children draw their own cookie shapes and compare the areas.

 Box Bases

Overview
In this lesson, children first predict and then determine the number of tiles or cubes needed to cover the bases of a variety of boxes or box lids. They compare the range of their estimates and discuss their actual results.

Materials
❖ boxes and/or box lids such as stationery boxes, large jewelry boxes, children's shoeboxes, or cosmetics boxes, at least 1 per pair of students (**Note:** Ask parents to help collect box lids and/or boxes.)
❖ tiles or cubes, 1 inch or 1 centimeter, at least 30 per pair of students
❖ *Box Bases* recording sheets, 1 per pair of students (see Blackline Masters)
❖ bags or containers, large enough to hold 30 tiles or cubes, 1 per pair of students

Vocabulary: area, base, biggest, bottom, cover, flat, inside, largest, row, side, smallest

Instructions

1. Before class, number the boxes and/or box lids and put the tiles or cubes into containers or bags.

2. To begin the lesson, ask the class to think about boxes that are used every day. Show the children several boxes and/or box lids. Discuss the meaning of the word *base*. Place the bottom of a box on the palm of your hand to indicate what you mean. Another way you can define the base is to cut the bottom out of a box and place the bottomless box on an overhead projector. Ask the children to think about which of the box bases seems to be the biggest and which one appears to be the smallest.

3. Discuss possible ways to measure the area of the bases. For example, students could place two bases in direct comparison with one another, they could trace the bases on graph paper and count the units inside the tracings, or they could cover the bases with tiles or cubes.

4. Pass around a box top with one tile or cube inside of it and ask students to predict or make a guess about how many tiles or cubes they think would be needed to cover the base. Discuss the range of guesses.

5. Model covering the box base with tiles and highlight the importance of careful placement. Tell the class that extra spaces should appear only at the edges, not in between the tiles. Explain that you are going to position the tiles or cubes in rows. Create the first row and count the tiles or cubes. Speculate with the children about the number of rows that will be needed to cover the area. Mention that extra space may show at the edges and explain that for the purposes of this lesson, only whole tiles will be recorded.

6. Cover the rest of the base, stopping at intervals to allow children to revise their estimates. Record the total number of tiles or cubes actually used.

7. Provide partners with one box or box lid, a bag of materials, and one recording sheet. Tell them to make a prediction about how many tiles or cubes the box or lid will hold and then check to see how many actually fit in it. Have children trade and determine the area for several different boxes or box lids.

8. During a whole-class discussion, ask students to show the boxes that had the largest area, the smallest area, and any two that had the same area.

Extension

◈ Select one of the boxes that had significant fractional remainders at the edges of the base. Instead of ignoring the remainders, have students measure the area using paper squares that can be cut, rather than tiles or cubes, to determine the total area of the base.

◈ Personal Flags

Overview

In this lesson each child arranges 1-inch paper squares, cut in half or left whole, on a 4-by-6-inch rectangle to create a personal flag. When the flags are complete, students discuss them in terms of pattern and area.

Materials

◈ flags or pictures of flags from a resource like *Firefly Guide to Flags Around the World* (2003), at least 6

◈ 4-by-6-inch paper, white unlined, 1 per student

◈ 1-inch paper squares, in multiple colors such as red, blue, yellow, green, and purple, 24 per child

Vocabulary: area, cover, greatest, half, least, less than half, more than half, most, space

Instructions

1. Begin by asking the children, "What do you know about flags? Where do you see them?" Very likely children will remember seeing the flag outside of the school, at sporting events, in front of the post office, or in front of restaurants. Explain that countries and states use flags as symbols (refer to the written resource on flags and the Olympics). Have children look carefully at your collection of flags or pictures of flags and discuss the shapes and colors that they see.

2. Tell the students that each of them will make a flag using colors that they like. Show them the 4-by-6-inch white paper and the different colors of 1-inch squares. Explain that if they wish they may cut the squares into two pieces or leave them whole. Model how to make a paper flag. Select a small square, fold it in half to form two rectangles, and cut on the fold. Do the same with another square. Select one or two more squares but leave them whole. Place the pieces haphazardly on a piece of white paper, allowing some of them to overlap. Explain to the students why this is not a good arrangement. Then rearrange the squares and half-squares on the white paper, being careful not to overlap any pieces. If you have not covered more than half the white rectangle, add more pieces. Once you are satisfied with your arrangement, glue the pieces onto the white paper. Ask students to describe the flag you have made.

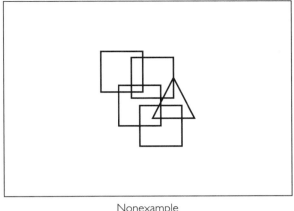

Nonexample

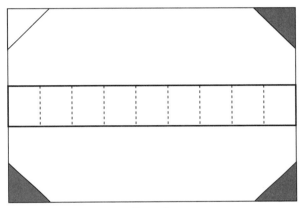

Example

3. Pass out the white papers for the flag backgrounds and make sure that children put their names on the *back* of the paper. Then, allow small groups of children to select pieces for their flags from a central location or set up several materials stations so that students can self-select their materials.

4. Now, give the students time to make their flags. Remind them to cover more than half the white rectangle and not to overlap pieces. As children complete their flags, have them record the colors that they used and the color that covered the greatest (most) area. This information can be recorded on a separate piece of paper or in math journals.

5. Have partners or small groups of students compare their flags and identify two ways that they are alike and two ways that they are different.

6. During a whole-class discussion, have children talk about how their flags are alike and different. Ask questions such as

   • Whose flag has at least half the area covered with the same color? How do you know?
   • What are the most colors anyone used to make his or her flag? The least?

- Which flags have an odd number of colors? Which flags have an even number of colors?
- Does anyone have a flag with a repeating pattern?
- Does anyone have a flag with symmetry?

7. Create a class book with the flags or display the flags on a class bulletin board so that children can look at them at talk about them over time.

Extension

❖ Have the children make larger flags with more colors and a variety of geometric shapes.

 ## Is It Half?

Overview

Students create a picture or design by coloring in selected squares on a grid-paper rectangle. They then estimate whether more than half, less than half, or exactly half of the area has been colored in and check their predictions by counting the squares.

Materials

❖ half-inch grid-paper rectangles, either 2 by 2 inches, 2 by 3 inches, 3 by 4 inches, or 4 by 4 inches, 1 per student
❖ crayons, 1 per student
❖ *Is It Half?* recording sheets, 1 per student (see Blackline Masters)

Vocabulary: compare, design, exactly, grid, half, large, larger, largest, less, more, rectangle, small, squares

Instructions

1. Show the children one of the half-inch grid-paper rectangles. Ask them to describe what they see. Together count the small squares within the grid.

2. Demonstrate how to create a picture or design by coloring some squares on a grid. Using a pencil, lightly mark the squares you plan to color. Then color them. Ask the students if they think that less than half, exactly half, or more than half of the small squares in your grid have been colored. Discuss ways to find out. Record the number of squares that you have colored and the number of squares that you have left blank, and compare those amounts. Ask the children if the numbers surprised them, or if they were about what they expected.

For example, if the colored area and the blank area are about even in number, does the white empty space appear to be greater? Discuss what each of the categories—less than half colored in, half colored in, more than half colored in—would look like in a design.

3. Tell the children that each of them will create a picture or design on a grid. Ask them to think about whether they want less than half, exactly half, or more than half of the squares in their grid to be colored in when they complete the design.

4. Distribute a paper rectangle, a crayon, and a recording sheet to each student. Set a time limit for the coloring, such as fifteen minutes. When the pictures or designs are complete, have children determine whether they colored less than half, exactly half, or more than half of the small squares in their grid. Have them record the number of squares they colored and the number of squares they left blank beneath their grids on the recording sheet. (See Figure 3–1.)

5. Tell children to trade designs. Have partners check the square count for accuracy and discuss inconsistencies until the count is correct.

6. During a whole-class discussion, ask the children how they determined if more than half, exactly half, or less than half of the grid was colored. Select a couple of

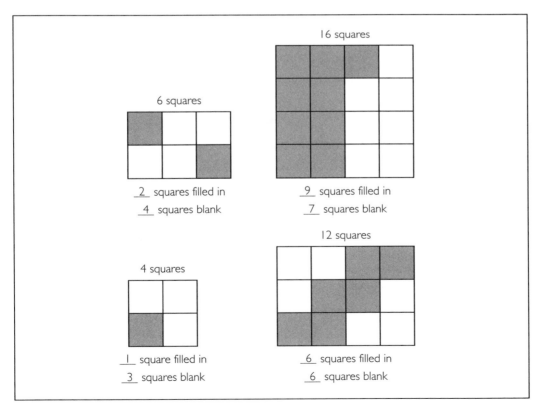

Figure 3–1 *For the* Is It Half? *activity, students recorded the number of squares filled in and left blank.*

grids, cover up the recorded amounts, ask children to predict how many squares are colored in, and then reveal the actual count. Ask if they are surprised and, if so, why. Another option is to select two grids that look different from one another but have the same number of squares colored in and discuss the count and ask the children if they would make the same predictions for both of the rectangles.

7. Create a bulletin board. Make three columns, each with one of the following labels: *Less Than Half Colored*, *Exactly Half Colored*, and *More Than Half Colored*. Have children post their designs in the appropriate place.

Extensions

❖ Offer a variety of grid sizes so that the level of difficulty can be adjusted for your students.

❖ Have each student create a picture and then ask a partner to determine how much area is colored in.

❖ Have students represent the colored and blank portions as a fractional amount, for instance, six out of ten squares are colored in and four out of ten remain blank.

 ## Surface Comparisons

Overview

During this lesson, students compare surface areas of common classroom objects that have rectangular shapes. Children use a variety of unit sizes to cover the rectangular surfaces and then discuss the similarities and differences of those unit sizes.

Materials

❖ bag containing several rectangular classroom objects such as blocks, chalkboard erasers, and books

❖ tiles, cubes, and paper squares, enough so that several students can use the same material, approximately 30 units per pair of students

Vocabulary: big, bigger, biggest, centimeter, count, cover, estimate, flat, inch, measure, predict, same, size, small, smaller, smallest, square, surface, unit

Instructions

1. To begin, show the class the bag that contains rectangular classroom objects.

2. Have several children take turns pulling items out of the bag. Discuss how many surfaces each item has; then ask the class to identify the one with the largest rectangular surface.

3. Explain that surfaces are usually measured using square units. Show children the measuring materials—the tiles, cubes, and paper squares. Emphasize that when measuring, it is very important to use the same-size unit; for example, if you decide to use centimeter cubes, you use only centimeter cubes and don't switch to inch cubes.

4. Hold up one of the objects from the bag for everyone to see. Identify the unit that will be used as the measurement tool, and ask children to predict the number of units that will be needed to cover the surface of the object. List some of the estimates and then have the class count with you as you carefully cover each surface of the object with the unit you've selected.

5. Explain to the students that they will be locating rectangular surfaces around the room and taking some measurements with a partner. Organize children into pairs and ask them to select a unit to measure their rectangular surfaces with. Have students record the following on a piece of paper:

   • the object they measured
   • the type of unit they used
   • how many units they used

6. After the measuring has been completed, lead a whole-class discussion. Ask partners who used the same type of unit to report their recorded results. After the results from each type of measuring unit have been shared, discuss similarities and differences relating to unit size, such as:

   • Who used the smallest unit? What was it?
   • How many units did you need?
   • Who used the largest unit?
   • What did you use and how many did it take to cover your object?
   • Why are the numbers different?

   Ask if any groups had remainders, or extra space that was not covered by their measuring units. Discuss the methods that children used for managing approximations, such as ignoring extra amounts, counting partial units, or combining the parts to create whole units. Compare the unit counts of the largest and smallest rectangles that students measured.

Extension

❖ Select one object to be measured and ask children to predict how many square centimeters would be needed to measure the surface area of the object and how many square inches would be needed to measure the same item. Then measure with each unit. Discuss the differences between the actual measurements. Compare the actual measurements with the children's predictions.

Compared with Your Hand

Overview

In this lesson, students compare the sizes of various classroom objects with that of their hands. Children use the language of size comparisons and encounter the idea that a hand can be larger than one object and at the same time smaller than another.

Materials

❖ *Compared with Your Hand* recording sheets, 1 per student (see Blackline Masters)

Vocabulary: about the same, area, bigger, compares, flat, larger than, smaller, smaller than, surface

Instructions

1. Hold up your hand and ask the children to look around the room for three things that seem to be smaller than your hand. Show the class a recording sheet and list their suggestions in the appropriate section.

   Show three things that are smaller than your hand:
   1.
   2.
   3.

   Show three things that are bigger than your hand:
   1.
   2.
   3.

   Next ask them to find three things that are bigger than your hand, and list these on the recording sheet.

2. Distribute the recording sheets, one to each child. Explain that each of them will find three objects in the classroom whose surface areas are smaller than their hand and three objects whose surface areas are larger than their hand. Tell students that they may record the information using pictures and/or words. Set a time limit and let the children know how you will cue them when the time is up.

3. As individuals get done, have them partner up and compare their recording sheets.

4. When everyone is ready, have children share their findings with the whole class. Ask, "What were some of the smallest objects that you compared with your hand? The largest? Which objects were almost the same length as your hand?"

Extension

❖ Have children draw and measure a handprint and other simple shapes. Then they can fill the areas with beans, count the beans, and compare the numbers required to fill each interior space.

 ## Handprint Wreath

Overview

In this lesson children make and collect a variety of cutout handprints. They compare the handprints, count them, and order them by size. Lastly, the class combines all of the handprints to create a decorative classroom wreath.

Materials

❖ paper cutout handprint samples, each a different size, 3
❖ different types of paper such as wallpaper, paper bags, newspapers, construction paper, and wrapping paper, 1 sample of each
❖ 5-by-5-inch paper, unlined white, 1 sheet per student
❖ note to parents, 1 per student (see Instruction 9)
❖ large poster board cut into a doughnut or wreath shape
❖ Lyrics to songs that involve counting fingers, such as "Five Little Monkeys Jumping on the Bed," or "Five Little Sparrows Sitting on a Wire"

Vocabulary: big, bigger, biggest, compare, large, larger, largest, order, small, smaller, smallest, tiny

Instructions

1. Before class, prepare three different-size paper cutout handprints as described in Instruction 5.

2. Begin the lesson with a familiar finger play such as *Five Little Monkeys Jumping on the Bed* or *Five Little Sparrows Sitting on a Wire*. After the song, ask each child hold up a hand and wiggle his or her fingers. Count the class's fingers by fives and then have children hold up both hands and count by tens.

3. Shift the conversation to the size of the students' hands. Remind the children that their hands were much smaller when they were born. Have each child make a fist to imagine the size of his or her hands as babies. Hold up your hand and compare it with a student's hand to give the class some idea of what their adult hands will look like.

4. Ask the children to close their eyes and picture the hands of people in their families. Have a few students identify the family member who has the largest hands

and the one who has the smallest hands. Explain that in class they will be making paper cutout handprints of their hands, and that for homework, they will help their families make handprints. Show the class the sample cutout handprints.

5. Demonstrate the process of creating a handprint by spreading your fingers and positioning your hand on a piece of paper. Trace around your fingers and then cut the handprint out. Describe the process as you work and acknowledge that cutting can be challenging.

6. Distribute the 5-by-5-inch paper and have everyone make a handprint. Encourage partners to help each other with both the tracing and the cutting. Circulate as children work, giving help where needed. As students complete the task, ask partners to discuss how their handprints compare.

7. After students have compared their handprints, have the class discuss the reasons—such as similarities in age—that their handprints are likely to be close in size.

8. Explain that for homework they will help their families create three different-size handprints to bring to class in the next few days. Tell students that the handprints can be made on paper of their choosing. Show the children your paper samples and encourage children to think about other interesting paper possibilities that their families might use.

9. If appropriate, have the children help compose a parent letter asking families to send contributions of three different-size handprints. (Or just write the letter yourself.) Include in the letter that the handprints will not be returned unless a special request is made. Also, include the date they are to be brought to school. Mention to the class that some families may not have enough people for three handprints, so perhaps those with large families could contribute more than three. Suggest that handprints be brought to the classroom in envelopes or zip-top bags.

10. As children begin to bring the handprints to school, tack them up on the bulletin board. Encourage children to look at them, compare them, and count both the hands and the fingers. The display provides practice and also reminds children to complete the homework assignment.

    Note: Help students who are not able to get this task accomplished at home gather handprints from available people at school, such as the principal, custodian, younger children, or older children.

11. Once the class has a sizable collection of handprints, have students organize them by size. Put the children into groups of three or four and then divide the class

Figure 3–2 *Students' handprint cutouts are arranged to form a classroom wreath during the* Handprint Wreath *activity.*

collection of handprints among them, making sure each group has a variety of sizes. Ask groups to order their handprints from the smallest to the largest.

12. Next ask the groups to place their handprints into three piles: small, medium, and large. Collect each group's pile, organizing them into three class piles so they are ready to be used in a final class project.

13. As a culminating activity, place the handprints in a circular arrangement on a doughnut-shaped piece of poster board. Glue or tape the largest handprints on the outside (fingers pointing out), the medium handprints in the center of the dough-nut shape, and the smallest handprints toward the interior. Handprints will over-lap in concentric circles, creating a wreath effect. (See Figure 3–2.) Display the wreath in the classroom so students can study it over time.

Extension

◈ Have children determine how many handprints have been brought into class. Then have them decide how many fingers there are altogether. Ask them to figure this out in more than one way, for example, by counting one at a time, making a table, drawing pictures, pattern counting with tallies, or using a 1–100 chart.

Decorative Tiles

Overview

This lesson focuses on area in the context of decorative floor tiles. Students are given the task of covering the area of a paper square "tile" with smaller squares. When everyone has made a tile, students compare and sort the tiles in different ways.

Materials

- 8-by-8-inch construction paper squares, in white only, 1 per student
- 2-by-2-inch construction paper squares, in four different colors, about 100
- 4-by-4-inch construction paper squares, in four different colors, about 50
- samples of geometric decorative ceramic floor tiles, 2 or 3 (see Instruction 1)
- samples of geometric decorative paper tiles, 2 or 3 (see Instruction 1)

Vocabulary: big, bigger, biggest, cover, decorative, estimate, geometric, large, larger, largest, length, overlap, size, small, smaller, smallest, square, surface, width

Instructions

1. Prior to the lesson, visit a flooring or hardware store to obtain two to three different decorative ceramic tiles. Also make two or three paper tile samples to show the class. Begin with a white 8-by-8-inch square. Select enough smaller colored squares to completely cover it. When you are satisfied with your arrangement, glue the small squares to the larger one. Use only 2-by-2-inch squares, only 4-by-4-inch squares, or a combination of both.

2. To begin the lesson, ask the children to name places where they have seen decorative floor tiles and to describe what they saw. Show the sample ceramic tiles to the class.

3. Tell the class to imagine that you have a tile store that sells decorative tiles. Explain that each of them will create a tile sample by covering a large white paper square with smaller colored squares. Show the class the paper samples you prepared ahead of time. (See Figure 3–3.)

4. Review the process of choosing the colors and sizes for a tile pattern. Explain that smaller squares need to completely cover the large white square and cannot overlap. Depending upon your students, and your glue supply, you may wish to remind the class how to place a *small* amount of glue on the white square before positioning a smaller square.

5. Discuss the area of your sample tile. Ask questions like, "How many colors were used on this tile? Which color covers the most area? Do any two colors cover the

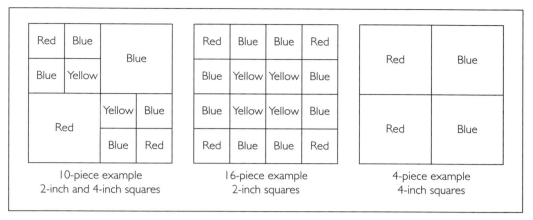

Figure 3–3 *Different colors of paper squares are arranged to create decorative floor tiles.*

same amount of area? How can we check to be sure?" Tell the children that these are the kinds of questions they will want to keep in mind as they create their own decorative tiles.

6. As you pass out the large white squares, have children put their names on the back of them. Encourage children to think about the small squares that they will choose. Ask them: "What colors appeal to you? Would you like to use the larger, four-by-four squares or the smaller, two-by-two squares or some of each? How many do you think you will need? Why do you think so?" Help the children get the needed materials. For efficiency, set up several supply stations in the room with the colored paper squares and give or glue sticks. When children have made their decisions and are ready to pick up their materials, allow only five or six students at each station at the same time.

7. As the children work, walk around the class and discuss the students' spatial arrangements. Encourage the children to identify which colors cover the most space and the least space. Discuss symmetrical arrangements and patterns.

8. When everyone has completed his or her sample, have students get together in a large group so that they can see the artwork displayed on the floor. Arrange the sample tiles in groups by similar attributes. For instance, place all of the tiles that used only 4-by-4-inch squares in one group, and then place the tiles that used only 2-by-2 squares in another group. Have the children guess why you arranged the tiles in this way. The next grouping pattern might be based upon the use of similar colors.

9. During a whole-class discussion, ask questions like the following:

   • How many 4-by-4-inch squares does it take to cover the large white square?
   • If we used only 2-by-2-inch squares, how many would we need to completely cover the tile?

- Did everyone use the same number of squares?
- How are these tiles alike? How are they different?
- How many people used exactly two colors? Three colors?

10. Finally, have each child write a number sentence that shows how many of each color he or she used (show them an example with the + symbol) and how many squares he or she used altogether.

Extensions

◈ Have students use different-size white squares, such as 16-by-16-inch squares.

◈ Invite a flooring expert to come for a visit and bring flooring samples and measurement tools along with other materials that are commonly used in this profession.

◈ Glue the children's flooring samples to a very large piece of paper, such as rolled bulletin board paper, and laminate it to create one large artistic decoration.

Capacity

Introduction

Almost all young children have spent time pouring water and other substances from one container into another, building with blocks, and helping with cooking projects. During this kind of exploratory play, they are developing awareness of three-dimensional space. This chapter builds on those real-life experiences and uses contexts such as "containers" in nature (birds' nests, for example), scooping materials and filling different-size containers, children's literature, creating and filling origami cups, cooking with standard units of measurement, and creating block buildings to extend students' understanding of capacity and volume.

The lessons in this chapter engage children with problem situations that encourage them to make predictions, estimate, keep track of quantities, fill interior spaces, and consider the dimension of height. In a variety of ways, the lessons require students to order and compare amounts and to communicate their thinking and reasoning.

 Natural Containers

Overview

Children discuss different animals and the space they need to live in. They then draw pictures of living things in their natural homes, arrange them in size order, and create a class book.

Materials

❖ large pictures or clip art of animals in their natural homes (or containers)
❖ crayons, enough for the class to share

Vocabulary: big, fit, greatest, huge, in between, inside, just right, large, little, medium, regular, room inside, small, space

Instructions

1. In advance, prepare a variety of large pictures of living things in containers, such as a bird in a nest, a bee in honeycomb, a bear in a cave, a butterfly emerging from a chrysalis, and a chick next to an egg.

2. Discuss the idea that nature provides some special containers for living things and their families. Invite the children to sit close enough so they can look carefully at the pictures of the living things and their settings. Discuss how the various settings are alike and how they are different. Ask the children how each setting meets the needs of the particular animal and what they notice about the size of the animal and the size of its home, or container.

3. With the class, gather additional information about other living things and their settings from the Internet and/or from library resources. Tell the children that

each of them will contribute a page for a class book by drawing a living thing in its setting. Explain that when the pages are done, you will ask them whether the size and setting of their animal are small, large, or in between. With the class, generate a list of possibilities for student pictures. Include insects, birds, and animals that are native to your area, for example, chipmunks, mice, deer, and snakes. Distribute paper and crayons to the students and give them time to create their drawings.

4. When the pages are complete, ask students whether the natural containers or settings that they drew are actually small, medium, or large in the real world. Sort the pages according to these size categories and put them in the book in that order.

5. Share the book with the whole class and discuss how many of the animal settings represented in the book have actually been seen by someone in the class. Discuss which ones exist in your geographic area.

Extensions
◈ Have children find out more about an animal's habitat. Have them investigate what animals need in their habitats in addition to shelter.
◈ Visit a zoo online or in your area and find out how zoos have changed in the last thirty years in an effort to create habitats rather than shelters. Discuss the differences between a habitat and a shelter.

 ## The Right Fit

Overview
In this lesson children look closely at familiar containers and objects and then decide which object will fit in which container. Once done, students use ordinal numbers to identify the relative size of each box and object.

Materials
◈ opaque containers that vary in size, such as department store boxes, plastic and paper shopping bags, purses, and backpacks, 5
◈ objects of varying sizes that fit in the containers, such as costume jewelry, silk flowers, food, stuffed animals, 5
◈ tray or display area for the objects
◈ master list of what was in the boxes, bags, or containers
◈ *The Right Fit* recording sheets, 1 per student (see Blackline Masters)

Vocabulary: big, bigger, biggest, fifth, fill, first, fourth, inside, last, medium, second, small, smaller, smallest, space, third

Instructions

1. Put the five containers of varied sizes on display so that the class can easily see them. Ask the children what they think the containers are used for.

2. Show the students the five objects that vary in size from small to large. Explain that one of the objects belongs in each container. Ask the children how they might decide which object should be placed in which container.

3. Children usually match the smallest and largest items with the smallest and largest containers very quickly. Ask the children why this happens. Place those two items inside their containers and then look at the remaining three objects. Ask the children which container they should fill next and why. Continue until all five items have been placed in the appropriate containers.

4. Reveal your master list and check to see if it matches the results of the class discussion.

5. On their recording sheets, have the children draw pictures of the containers as they correspond to each ordinal number: 1st, 2nd, 3rd, 4th, and 5th. Have children fold the paper the long, "hot dog" way on the solid line with the numbers and pictures on the outside, then cut on the dotted lines, creating five sections, one for each ordinal number. Inside the numbered flip pages, suggest students draw pictures of the objects that went in the containers.

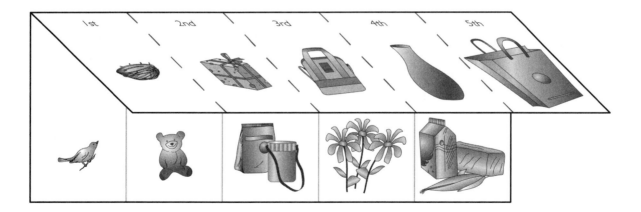

Extension

❖ Invite students to create their own ordered sets of objects for the containers by bringing in objects from home or using objects from the classroom.

◈ It's in the Bag

Overview

In this lesson, children make old-fashioned paper bag characters, similar to puppets, and consider the question How full is the paper bag?

Materials

- ◈ envelope, 1
- ◈ small paper sacks, such as lunch bags, 1 per student
- ◈ packing materials such as scrunched-up newspaper or tissue paper, enough to stuff each small paper sack
- ◈ large paper bags, 4
- ◈ crayons in various colors, enough for the class to share
- ◈ markers in various colors, enough for the class to share
- ◈ optional: construction paper in different colors, at least 12 large sheets

Vocabulary: about half full, empty, estimate, fill, full, in, less than half full, more than half full

Instructions

1. Prior to the lesson, set up at least one materials and stapling center where children can obtain craft materials needed to create their characters (e.g., construction paper, crayons, glue, staplers). Place the tissue paper and/or newspaper for stuffing the small paper sacks in large paper bags that can be passed around the room as children need them.

2. Begin the lesson by holding up a piece of paper, an envelope, and a paper bag to help children get the idea of three-dimensional space as opposed to two-dimensional space. Ask the children how the piece of paper, the envelope, and the bag are alike and how they are different. Develop the idea that envelopes and bags have space inside and are types of containers. Have the class name other examples of paper, plastic, wood, or metal containers.

3. Explain to the class that during this lesson, partners will use the small paper bags to make paper bag characters. Let students decide what type of character they would like to make or suggest specific topics or literary characters that are being studied in class.

4. Materials can be kept simple, with few choices such as crayons and markers, or can be more elaborate, with construction paper shapes or craft store materials.

Show the children the basic procedures for drawing or gluing a face on the paper sack. Explain that the drawing needs to be done before the paper bag is stuffed.

5. Demonstrate how to gently stuff the bag with packing material. Show the children that this could be done in several ways:
   • packing the sack less than half full
   • packing the sack about halfway full
   • packing the sack until it is almost full
   Discuss the vocabulary listed above and create examples of all three possibilities.

less than half full

halfway full

almost full

6. Distribute the small paper bags and remind children about the location of extra art supplies. When children have completed the artwork for their characters, tell them to pass around the bags of stuffing materials and, after stuffing their bags, have them stapled at the materials center.

7. After the puppets have been stuffed and the work areas have been cleaned up, ask students to record in their math notebooks, or on a scrap piece of paper, how fully their characters are stuffed. If there's time, have partners share their recordings.

8. When everyone has made a character, put the characters on display and have the children help you place them into the categories: almost full, half full, and less than half full. Compare the numbers of characters in the three categories. Discuss what it means for something to be full.

Extensions
◈ Children could determine other criteria by which to sort the puppet characters.
◈ Use large paper bags to make a family of characters. Have students give them names and write stories about them.

How Many Scoops?

Overview

In this lesson, children estimate how many scoops of some small item a jar will hold and then find the actual amount. They experiment twice, each time using a different-size scoop.

Materials

◈ large clear plastic cylindrical jar, such as a peanut butter jar
◈ plastic bag filled with red beans, popcorn, or lentils, enough to fill the jar
◈ different-size scoops or measuring cups, in different colors if possible, 2
◈ large rubber band

Vocabulary: check, estimate, fewer, guess, half full, inside, less, measure, measuring cup, more, predict, same number, $\frac{1}{2}$ cup, 1 cup

Instructions

1. Begin the lesson by inviting the children to sit close to you so that they can see the materials. Hold up the jar and ask the children what it might have been used for. Show the class the two scoops or measuring cups and ask them to point to the larger of the two. Select one of the scoops to fill the jar with beans, popcorn, or lentils.

2. Explain that your plan is to fill the scoop as evenly as possible and empty it into the jar until the container is full. After pouring a few scoops into the jar, stop scooping, and ask the children to think about how many scoops it will take to fill the jar all the way to the top. Tell students to raise their hands when you mention the number that matches their guess. Ask, "Do you think two scoops will fill the jar? Three? Four? Five? Six? Seven? Eight? Nine? Ten? More than ten?" Resume filling the jar. Have the children count the scoops as you do this.

3. When the jar is about half full, stop again. Ask the class if anyone would like to change his or her guess now that the container is about half full and everyone has a little more information. Place the rubber band around the jar at the halfway point (see page 90, top). Discuss the idea of *half full* and mention the number of scoops that are in the jar as you position the rubber band. Ask students how many scoops they think will be needed to fill the remaining half of the jar. Explain that it is a good thing to make better guesses as you are able to do so. Have students think about whether or not their guesses or estimates have changed since the beginning of the lesson. Ask, "What new information might help you revise your guess?"

4. When everyone is ready, continue to fill the jar. Have the class count the rest of the scoops. Write down the final number of scoops used to fill the jar. Ask, "Was the number close to what you expected? If not, why?"

5. Now, hold up the second scoop and compare it once again with the first. Empty the contents of the jar back into the plastic bag and repeat steps 2–4 using the second scoop. Write down the final number of scoops.

6. Compare the final amounts. Do the following in a class discussion:
   - Ask the children to look at the number of the first scoop and the number of the second scoop needed to fill the jar and discuss why the numbers are different.
   - Have students describe size differences between the measuring scoops.
   - Make a list of math words used during the activity such as *fill, size, same, bigger, smaller, amount, more, less,* and *count.*
   - Ask the class to make some statements about the experiment. It may help to use a sentence starter such as "We used two different-size scoops to fill a jar with beans and we noticed . . ."

   Children will be at various points in their understandings about the relationship between the scoop size and the volume of the jar. All of the students will benefit from hearing the language and reasoning of their classmates.

Extension
❧ Make the materials available for children to use independently, for instance, in a center.

◈ What Unit Did You Use?

Overview

This lesson offers hands-on opportunities for children to fill containers using more than one unit of measurement. Students keep track of the number of units that it takes to fill a container with two different-capacity scoops and then compare their results.

Materials

- ◈ clean reusable clear plastic household containers in different sizes and shapes, 2 per pair of students
- ◈ bags filled with a pouring material such as sand, lentils, or rice, 1 per pair of students
- ◈ large, shallow cardboard box lids, 1 per pair of students
- ◈ index cards showing the symbols of 1 cup, $\frac{1}{2}$ cup, and 1 tablespoon, 1 set per pair of students
- ◈ scoops with capacities of 1 cup, $\frac{1}{2}$ cup, and 1 tablespoon, 2 different scoops per pair of students
- ◈ *What Unit Did You Use?* recording sheets, 1 per student (see Blackline Masters)
- ◈ optional: children's literature book that use examples of capacity such as *Pigs in the Pantry: Fun with Math and Cooking,* by Amy Axelrod (1997); *Everybody Cooks Rice,* by Norah Dooley (1991); and *Warthogs in the Kitchen: A Sloppy Counting Book,* by Pamela Duncan Edwards (1998)

Vocabulary: container, cup, different number, empty, fill, ingredients, measure, same number, scoop, tablespoon, $\frac{1}{2}$ cup

Instructions

1. Before class, number each of the clear plastic containers so that children can easily refer to the container they are working with. Then, prepare the cardboard box lids by placing in each one 1 bag of pouring material, 2 different scoops, 1 set of index cards, and 2 recording sheets. (**Note:** Box lids are more sturdy and stable than plastic bags and are easier for students to manage.)

2. Begin the lesson by showing the class the collection of numbered plastic containers. Ask the children to raise their hands if they have ever spent time filling and emptying containers of water or sand just for the fun of it. Call attention to the fact that these containers vary in size and shape. Hold up one of the containers and the 1-cup scoop and ask students how many scoops they think it will take to fill the container.

3. Next show the children the ½-cup scoop and the 1-tablespoon scoop. Ask students which of the three scoops they would choose to use to fill the container. Have students point to their choice. Ask a few students to explain the reasons for their choices. For example, one student might say, "I would pick the *one-cup* measure, because it will take too many scoops to use the *tablespoon*." Another student might say, "I think I would use the middle one (half cup) so nothing would spill out." Someone else might say, "I'd use more than one kind. Like the one-cup scoop and the tablespoon." Accept the responses and explain that today's activity will help them become more familiar with common cooking measures.

4. Show the children the prepared box lids containing the pouring materials, scoops, index cards, and recording sheets. Explain that each of them will work with a partner to do some pouring with the scoops that are in the boxes. Tell the class that you expect partners to share the jobs so that the work is fair and that both partners do some pouring and some recording.

5. Write the following directions on the board. Discuss them.
   a. Choose a scoop.
   b. Make a prediction about how many scoops will fill your first container.
   c. Fill the container.
   d. Complete the recording sheet.
   e. Repeat steps 1 through 4 with the second scoop.
   f. Repeat the whole process with your second container.

6. Show the class that the names or labels for the measurements are written right on the cups or spoons. Remind everyone to use the index cards if they need help with the written and symbolic forms of the measurement when completing their recording sheets.

7. Pass out one box lid and two containers to each pair of students. Give them plenty of time to fill the containers and record the results. Assist children with using level scoops of their pouring material if necessary. Note the strategies students utilize to keep track of the number of scoops they're using.

8. After the materials have been put away, have a whole-group discussion. Ask students to talk about their experience and describe the unit they would recommend for measuring their containers.

9. As an option before or after the lesson, books such as *Pigs in the Pantry, Everybody Cooks Rice,* and *Warthogs in the Kitchen* can be used to develop mathematical awareness that specific units of measurement help people keep track of amounts. Each of these books includes recipes at the end extending the real-life cooking

context. Reference to television cooking shows can also provide a common starting point for this lesson.

Extension

❖ Ask some people in food service or the medical profession to come for a visit to discuss how they use this kind of measurement in their work.

 Hats and Mittens

Overview

A story about hats or mittens sets the stage for this lesson, which focuses on spatial visualization. Students play a guessing game in which they decide which objects fit in a hat or mitten and which don't; then they create a class book that illustrates their reasoning.

Materials

❖ book about hats or mittens such as *Caps for Sale*, by Esphyr Slobodkina (1985); *Hats, Hats, Hats*, by Ann Morris (1989); or *The Mitten*, by Jan Brett (1989)

❖ picture of hat or mitten

❖ hat or mitten

Vocabulary: big, fill, fit, greatest, inside, least, left, little, right, room, space, three-dimensional, two-dimensional

Instructions

1. Create a context for discussing interior space by reading a story about hats or mittens. Discuss whether the story is fiction or nonfiction. Both *The Mitten* and *Caps for Sale* are based upon traditional folktales. *Hats, Hats, Hats*, by contrast, includes photographs of people wearing hats in many settings throughout the world.

2. Have the children discuss the purposes for hats or mittens. Ask questions such as these:
   • Who wears them and why?
   • Does everyone wear them?
   • When do people wear them?
   • Are they all the same size?

• What are they made of?
• Who makes them?

Also ask the children what questions the story makes them think of.

3. Show the class a picture of a hat or a mitten and the actual hat or mitten. Ask the children to talk with a partner about how the picture and the real thing are alike and how they are different; then share ideas with the large group. Demonstrate what they describe using the interior space of the hat or mitten. Introduce the terms *two-dimensional* and *three-dimensional* space.

4. Play a game with the class in which everyone thinks of things that could fit inside the hat (or mitten). Begin by suggesting an object in the classroom. If the students believe that the object will fit in the hat, they signal with thumbs up. If the students think the object can't fit in the hat, they signal with thumbs down. Continue the game as long as the class desires. At first, select objects from the classroom because you can actually check if there is disagreement. Then move on to objects such as a tricycle, a toothbrush, a microwave oven, and a spoon, and have children add to the list.

5. After playing the game, have each child make a page for a class book, titled *Will It Fit?* Give each child a sheet of paper. Give the following directions:
   a. Fold the paper in half (the class can decide whether it will be the hot dog way or the hamburger way).
   b. On the left side, draw a picture of something that can fit inside a hat (or mitten).
   c. On the right side of the paper, draw a picture of something that is definitely too big to fit inside a hat (or mitten).

Extensions

❖ Have partners think of ideas for two categories: containers and objects. Then have them share their thinking using this format:

A _____ will fit, but a _____ won't.

For example, "one partner might say, "my lunch will fit in my lunchbox" and the other partner could respond with a counterpoint, "a picnic for the class will not." Or, "two classes can fit in a school bus for a field trip," and "the whole school cannot."

❖ Instead of having one student name the container and another, the object, increase the level of difficulty by having each student think of both the container and the object. In addition, have students record their comparisons, illustrate them, and create individual or class booklets.

⬙ Making Gorp

Overview

In this lesson, children prepare a nutritious snack that engages them in measuring cupfuls of familiar ingredients. They then estimate how many gallon-size bags will be needed to store the snack until it is time to eat it.

Materials

- ❖ large bowl
- ❖ measuring cup, 1-cup capacity
- ❖ zip-top bags, gallon size, about 20
- ❖ ladle
- ❖ plastic cups, 1 per student
- ❖ chart paper, 1 sheet

Some or all of the following, to make about thirteen 1-cup servings:

- ❖ miniature pretzels, at least 3 cups
- ❖ raisins, at least 2 cups
- ❖ breakfast cereal such as Kix or Cheerios, at least 2 cups
- ❖ granola, at least 2 cups
- ❖ peanuts, at least 2 cups
- ❖ M&M's, at least 2 cups

Vocabulary: equal parts, estimate, fill, gallon, keep track, mix, scoops, 1-cup capacity

Instructions

1. Before class, do the following:

   - Find out about any food allergies that your students may have so you can adjust the recipe accordingly.
   - Create a large visual of the recipe on chart paper by writing *Amount: 1 cup*, drawing a 1-cup measuring cup, and listing the ingredients you have decided to use. (**Note:** The amount may vary depending on your class size.)
   - Elicit room parents or volunteers to help organize the event. Ask each volunteer to contribute one ingredient, which you assign, or give one person the recipe and the responsibility of arranging for others to send in needed ingredients.

2. On the day of the lesson, assemble the ingredients and post the recipe where every child can see it. Begin the lesson by telling the children they will be making a treat called gorp, and establish some basic routines for cooking, such as hand washing.

3. After reviewing the recipe, have children take turns pouring an ingredient into the measuring cup and then into the large bowl. With each addition, stir the mixture.

4. When the recipe has been completed, show children a gallon-size zip-top bag. Ask them to predict how many gallon-size bags the contents of the bowl will fill.

5. After discussing their estimates, use a ladle to fill the bags and have the children keep track of the number used. Ask, "How many students can be served from the bags of gorp? How many cups will be needed for each person to have a cup of Gorp to eat?"

6. Use plastic cups to share and enjoy the Gorp with another class. If appropriate, invite older class buddies with whom your students read or play math games to come to your classroom and share the snack.

Extension
◈ Have a parent volunteer help to put together a favorite family recipe book for your class.

 Origami Cups

Overview
In this lesson students create two different-size paper origami cups by making a series of simple folds. They then predict which will hold more and find out by filling each cup with cereal pieces.

Materials
◈ 5-by-5-inch colored copy paper or commercial origami paper, 1 square per student
◈ 7-by-7-inch colored copy paper or commercial origami paper, 1 square per student
◈ cereal that can be counted, such as Chex or Cheerios, 1 paper cup full per student
◈ large bowl
◈ 8-ounce paper cups, 1 or 2
◈ optional: *Origami Cup* directions (see Blackline Masters)
◈ optional: chart paper

Vocabulary: cup, fold, full, hold, inside, less, more, origami, square, triangle

Instructions

1. Prior to the lesson, make two sample origami cups as described in Instruction 4. Fill the large bowl with the cereal.

2. Begin the lesson by showing the children one of the sample origami cups that you made. Explain that you made the cup using a Japanese paper-folding method called *origami*. Tell the children that they will each make two origami cups and then check to see how much each holds.

3. Hold up two different-size squares of paper and ask students what they notice about them. Have the children make some predictions about what will happen when the two squares are folded into cups. Ask, "How will the cups be alike? How will they be different?" Write their responses on chart paper or the board.

4. Pass out the larger of the two squares. When everyone is ready, give the following directions, modeling as you give each one:

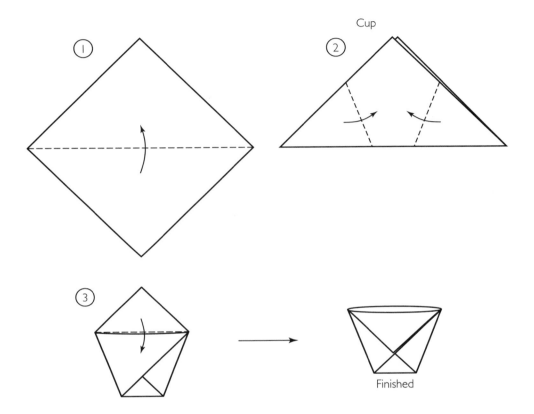

Cup

Finished

a. Fold the square so that you have a triangle.
b. Place the long folded side of the triangle at the bottom and the point at the top.
c. Fold one of the side points of the triangle up to touch the opposite side like a wing folding in or an arm folding (see diagram).
d. Fold the other side in a similar way. (Origami creases are usually very deep, holding shapes in place. At this point the children may wish to use a little bit of tape to hold them in place, because their creases will not be very strong.)
e. Fold the top triangles down over each side of the cup.

Have children who need help completing the cup partner up with a classmate who has completed the task successfully. (**Note:** If you want, you can hand out copies of the folding directions to the students as well.)

5. Distribute the smaller squares and repeat the process. (**Note:** You can make the lesson simpler by doing one cup one day and the other the next day).

6. Review the children's predictions about what would happen with the different-size squares when they were folded into the cup shapes. Explain to the children that they are going to find out exactly how much the cups hold by filling each one with cereal. Tell them that they are to keep track of the number of pieces of cereal that they place in their cups. Suggest that they count each piece of cereal as they put it into the cup and when the cup is full, record the number of pieces of cereal on a piece of paper. Alternatively, they can fill up the cup with cereal, dump the cereal out, and then count the pieces.

7. Use an 8-ounce paper cup as a scoop and make the cereal available to the children by placing it on clean sheets of paper in their work areas. Children can count pieces of cereal as they place them in their cups.

8. When everyone is ready, lead a class discussion. Ask questions like "How much cereal fit in your small cup? How much does your cup hold when it is full? Did anyone else have the same amount? How much cereal fit in your large cup? Did anyone else have the same amount? Which cup held less?" On the board, record the range and frequency of numbers that the children have counted.

8	9	10	11	12	13	14	15
I	II	IIII		II		II	I
I	I	III		I		I	
						I	

range: 8–15
mode: 10

Ask the children to look at the information and discuss what they notice, for example, the fewest, the most, the most frequent, the range.

Extensions
◈ Show children the variety of paper squares and ask them to choose a square that represents the size cup they want to make. Explore the question "Can you make a cup using your square that is the same size as the teacher's example or one that is twice as big?"
◈ Have students use measuring cups and predict, then find out, the amounts that the origami cups can hold. For example, do children think that the amount of cereal they have in the small origami cup is closer to $\frac{1}{4}$ cup or $\frac{1}{2}$ cup?

 ## Baking Cookies

Overview
Baking cookies with young children is a very natural context for investigating measurement and capacity. This lesson includes reading a recipe, measuring ingredients, making the cookies, counting them, and, of course, eating them.

Materials

- cookie recipe (see Instructions)
- cookie recipe, listed and illustrated on chart paper
- ingredients as indicated in the recipe
- clear measuring cups that show the markings for $\frac{1}{4}, \frac{1}{3}, \frac{1}{2}, \frac{2}{3}, \frac{3}{4}$, and 1 cup, 1 or 2
- measuring spoons, 1 or 2 sets
- mixing spoons, at least 2
- bowls, at least 2
- baking pans, at least 2
- paper towels, at least 1 roll
- pot holders, at least 2
- spatulas, at least 1
- timers, at least 1
- optional: a little music to add to the fun

Vocabulary: combine, cup, degrees, half cup, ingredients, measure, recipe, teaspoon, timer

Instructions

1. Before class, decide on procedures for having children wash their hands prior to baking and decide on how you want them to rotate through the cooking area, what they should do in the cooking area, and what they should do when they are not involved in cooking.

    Choose one of the following cookie recipes, which have been successfully used in classrooms, or ask parents to send in simple recipes. Assemble the necessary ingredients and tools.

Old-Fashioned Crisp Oatmeal Cookies

1 cup shortening (Crisco, margarine, or butter)
2 cups brown sugar
2 beaten eggs
2 cups quick oatmeal
$1\frac{1}{2}$ cup flour
1 teaspoon baking soda
1 teaspoon cinnamon
1 teaspoon vanilla
$\frac{1}{2}$ teaspoon salt

Blend shortening and brown sugar.
Add eggs, oatmeal, flour, baking soda, cinnamon, vanilla, and salt.
Drop by teaspoonful on cookie sheet.
Bake until golden brown, 7 to 8 minutes at 375°.

Almond Butter Cookies

1 cup butter
$\frac{1}{2}$ cup sugar
$\frac{1}{4}$ teaspoon salt
1 teaspoon almond flavoring
2 cups flour

Blend butter and sugar.
Add the remaining ingredients.
Mix together.
Refrigerate from 1 to 24 hours.
Drop by teaspoonful on a cookie sheet.
Bake for 12 to 15 minutes at 350°.

Peanut Butter Crunchies (no-bake cookies)

$\frac{1}{4}$ cup sugar
$\frac{1}{4}$ cup light corn syrup
$\frac{1}{4}$ cup plus 2 tablespoons peanut butter
$\frac{1}{2}$ teaspoon vanilla
1 cup Special K cereal

Stir sugar and syrup together and heat to boiling in a saucepan.
Remove from heat and add peanut butter, vanilla, and cereal.
Mix well and drop by spoonfuls onto waxed paper.

Grandma Ruby's Molasses Cookies

1 stick butter
1 cup sugar
1 egg
$\frac{1}{4}$ cup molasses
2 cups flour
2 teaspoons baking powder
1 teaspoon cinnamon
$\frac{1}{2}$ teaspoon cloves
$\frac{1}{2}$ teaspoon ginger
$\frac{1}{2}$ teaspoon salt

Cream together the butter and sugar. Add the egg and the molasses.
Combine or sift together the flour and baking powder. Add to the molasses
    mixture.
Add the remaining ingredients. Mix well and chill for at least 1 hour.
Form into 1-inch balls.
Place on greased cookie sheet 2 inches apart.
Bake 8 to 10 minutes at 375°.

2. Begin the lesson by playing a game of *Guess My Word*. Display a blank line for each letter in the word *cookies*: _ _ _ _ _ _ _. Tell the class that most of the letters in this particular word are vowels and that this word is a thing, or a noun. Have the children take turns guessing letters until they have spelled the word.

3. Once the children see the word, explain that they will be baking cookies in today's lesson so they can learn about measurement. Show and identify some of the measurement tools that will be used and display the large chart recipe. Define the word *ingredients*. With the class, look at the list of ingredients and have the children help identify the wet and the dry ingredients. Discuss the importance of using recipes; for example, they make it possible for cookies to look and taste the same each time you bake them.

4. Discuss procedures and expectations with the class. Rotate children through the cooking area so that everyone has some role in the process of making the cookies. (The actual baking can be done by a parent volunteer or at another time.)

5. As children follow along with the recipe, call attention to the measurement markings on the cups and spoons. Match the measurement markings in the recipe with the symbols on the measurement tools. Discuss comparisons between quantities such as $\frac{1}{2}$ cup and 1 cup and $\frac{1}{2}$ teaspoon and 1 teaspoon.

6. Count the cookies as they are placed on the cookie sheets. Discuss the number that is needed for everyone in the class to have one.

7. Read the final directions in the recipe and discuss the measurement ideas of cooking time and temperature.

8. As the children get ready to enjoy the cookies, ask them to try to list the ingredients from memory. Read the recipe together and discuss the amounts of the various ingredients. Have children try to determine what they can actually taste as they eat the cookies.

Extension

◈ Buy some cookies that come in different types of packages, for example, a bag of cookies and a cellophane-wrapped container of cookies in rows. Ask children to predict the number of cookies in each package. Discuss which one they would be more likely to buy and why. Have the class check the actual amounts of cookies in each container. Ask:

• Which container appeared to have more? Why?

• Did it have more? If so, how many more?

◈ Look-Alike Buildings

Overview

In this lesson, partners use a variety of building materials to create three-dimensional structures that are all the same size on the outside but are different on the inside.

Materials

◈ building materials such as geoblocks, cubes, Legos, pattern blocks, and Cuisenaire rods, 4 different kinds, at least 20 units per student

◈ half-inch grid paper, 1 sheet per pair of students (see Blackline Masters)

◈ optional: half-inch grid overhead transparency

Vocabulary: alike, amount of space, base, building, different, exactly, high, inside, interior, long, miniature, outside, same size, unique, wide

Instructions

1. Ask the children if they have ever been in a neighborhood where the houses look very much like each other. Tell them that the inside of those houses probably aren't the same at all. Explain that during the lesson, partners will make miniature buildings that are all the same size on the outside but are different on the inside. Show the children the building materials they can choose from. Tell the children that each building needs to be exactly as long, exactly as wide, and exactly as high as its partner building, but each needs to be made with a different kind of block.

2. Ask several children to repeat the directions in their own words and invite class members to ask clarifying questions. If needed, model the process of creating two "almost" matching buildings.

3. Show the class a piece of half-inch grid paper (or the transparency) and explain that the grid paper can be used as a mat to help make the bottom, or base, of both buildings exactly the same size.

4. If appropriate, have the class decide if it makes sense to set a limit for the number of blocks per building. It should be clear that the buildings must be three-dimensional, that is, they must have *height, length,* and *width*.

5. Help the children get settled with their materials and give partners sufficient time to create their buildings and compare them.

6. When everyone is ready, have students walk around the room and examine one another's work to look for similarities and differences between the buildings.

7. Lead a whole-class discussion. Encourage students to talk about the challenges of this task. Ask:

- Were you able to successfully make two buildings that looked alike but had different interiors?
- Were some materials better to use than others? Why?
- Do you have recommendations for others who may work on this task at another time?

Extension

◈ Have children continue to investigate this problem in a center or block corner that contains a variety of materials.

Weight

Introduction

Primary-age children can probably still remember being lifted into the air and carried around during their early years. Many of them have younger siblings that they lift and carry. Real-life applications of weight are filled with questions like What's heavy? What's light? Can I lift it? How far can I carry that?

In the lessons in this chapter students engage in direct comparisons of objects in a variety of ways and extend these early ideas to answer the following: Which one is heavier? How much heavier? Which one's lighter? How much lighter?

These lessons provide a number of different contexts for exploring the concept of weight, including comparing items found in nature, using balance scales, weighing books, creating mobiles, running relay games, and reading children's literature. Each of the lessons requires students to make predictions, estimate, listen to others, and explain their thinking.

Ordering Familiar Objects by Weight

Overview
In this lesson students use common classroom objects to clarify the language that is used to describe weight. Students order a series of objects by weight and discuss their results with a partner. The children also consider whether the order remains the same if size is the criteria, rather than weight.

Material
❖ classroom objects from the desk or cubby of each child, 5 per student

Vocabulary: big, bigger, biggest, heavier, heaviest, lighter, lightest, little, littler, littlest, small, smaller, smallest, weight

Instructions

1. Begin the lesson by asking if anyone can explain what it is that doctors and nurses are doing when they place babies on scales at the doctor's office. Ask: "What is the doctor checking?" Write on the board: *The doctor wants to see how much children _ _ _ _ _.* Fill in the letters for the word *weigh.* Also write the words *weight* and *measure* on the board. Discuss the definitions of these words. Encourage the children to provide multiple examples. For example, children might talk about family members watching their weight or measuring to see how much someone has grown.

2. Look around the classroom and play a game of I spy something heavy . . . and another game of I spy something light . . . to help establish the meaning of the words *heavy* and *light.*

3. Ask the children to think about the heaviest and lightest things inside their desks or cubbies. Have each child remove five objects and place them on top of his or her desk. Tell the students that their job is to put these objects in order from the lightest to the heaviest. Discuss ways that they could determine this. Children might suggest hefting two items to compare their weights or placing them on a balance scale to observe the comparison.

4. Have students record their objects in order of weight from lightest to heaviest.

5. When the objects have been ordered and recorded, have partners sitting next to each other check their lists for similarities and differences. Ask, "Did you choose any of the same items? Are the items in the same order?" Have partners heft each other's selections to see if they agree or disagree with the order in which they've been placed.

6. Next ask the children to reposition their objects in a new way. This time, instead of putting them in order by weight, they should order the objects by size. This may raise the question What does *size* mean? Allow each child to make the decision for him- or herself.

7. After children have placed and recorded their objects in this new order, ask questions such as "Is the order the same as when you arranged your objects by weight? Are the biggest things always the heaviest? Are the lightest things always the smallest? Are size and weight the same thing?"

8. Have a class discussion about the results of this activity. Ask the children if they were surprised by any of their results.

Extensions

❖ Have children create small collections of materials for classmates to order by weight.

❖ Have a scavenger hunt using three *heavy*, three *medium*, and three *lightweight* objects. See what interpretations children bring to these words.

 Balance Scales

Overview

In this lesson, students use pan balance scales to determine the weight of small lightweight objects. Ann Tompert's story *Just a Little Bit* uses a seesaw context to provide some background before the balance work begins.

Materials

❖ pan balance scales, 1 per group of three or four students

❖ cubes, tiles, teddy bear counters, and/or Cuisenaire rods, about 20 of one type per group

❖ sets of half a dozen different lightweight objects such as a toy car, a box of crayons, a stone, a marker, an old key, and a small toy, placed in small bags, 1 per group

❖ optional: *Just a Little Bit*, by Ann Tompert (1993)

Vocabulary: balance, counting words, heavier, less, lighter, little, more, opposite, side, weight

Instructions

1. If available, read *Just a Little Bit*, and have children describe the seesaw action. Ask the class: "What happens when all of the animals join in the fun?"

2. Introduce the materials:
   • Show the class one of the balance scales. Demonstrate how both sides of the scale move when pressure is applied.
   • Hold up the cubes, tiles, teddy bear counters, or Cuisenaire rods. Explain that these materials will be used as the unit of measure on one side of the scale.

3. Show the children how to find the weight of a lightweight object. Place one of the objects from a bag on one side of the scale. Place enough cubes, or another unit of measure, on the opposite side until the scale balances. Count the cubes and explain that the number of cubes tells how much the object weighs.

4. Pass out the materials and give groups of three or four students a few minutes to explore all of the materials. Ask them to predict which is the heaviest item and which is the lightest object in their bags.

5. Explain that the groups will need to measure the items from their bags by counting the number of cubes that it takes to balance them on the other side of the scale. As groups measure the objects, have them weigh each object; arrange the objects in order from the heaviest to the lightest; compare their results to their predictions; and record the specific results in terms of how many cubes each of the small objects weighed.

6. As you visit with groups, check to see if children understand the idea of *units of measure* being used on one side of the scale to balance the small lightweight objects placed on the other side. Discuss the differences between the small objects in the bags.

7. When everyone is done, have groups walk around the room to look at each other's results.

8. During a whole-class discussion, ask each group to report on its heaviest and lightest items and be prepared to demonstrate its findings. For example, one group may have found that a small car equaled four cubes; another group may have found that a key was equal to one cube. It's possible that two groups will report that different objects are equal to the same number of cubes. If this occurs, have the class directly compare the two objects on the scale. For example, both a car and a stone may equal two cubes. Use this opportunity to discuss the meaning of equality as a relationship rather than a sign that means "the answer is . . . "

Extensions

❖ Have each student draw a picture of a relationship that causes a scale to balance, for example, a toy car balancing four cubes.

❖ Have children pick two or more items and predict what they would weigh together. Then tell them to find the total weight and write a number sentence to represent their findings.

 ## Books and More Books

Overview

Each student selects two books in the classroom, predicts which is heavier, and then uses a hanger apparatus to check the prediction. Children also consider how weight and size are related.

Materials

❖ books of different weights, at least 2 per student
❖ large bags, 2 per pair of students
❖ hangers, 1 per pair of students
❖ large paper clips, 2 per pair of students
❖ optional: clothespins, 2 per pair of students

Vocabulary: big, bigger, biggest, different, dissimilar, heavier, heaviest, lighter, lightest, little, littler, littlest, small, smaller, smallest, weight

Instructions

1. Before class, assemble the hangers, bags, and paper clips (or clothespins) as shown, making one apparatus for each pair of students. Select two books of similar size but different weight for class demonstration.

2. Get the class's attention by holding up the prepared hanger device and the two books. Tell the children that you intend to use the hanger-bag scale to help you determine which book is heavier. Pose these questions as you compare the two books:
   - Are the biggest books always the heaviest?
   - Are the books with the most pages always the heaviest?
   - Are the smallest books always the lightest?
   - Are chapter books always the lightest?
   - Are books with colored pages heavier?
   - Are older books heavier?

3. Tell the class that each person will find two books in the room that seem to be of different or dissimilar weights. Then students will partner up and pairs will put all four of their books in order by weight. Explain that if questions arise during these comparisons, they are to use the hangers with the attached bags to check one book in relation to another.

4. Hand out a hanger scale to each pair and set the children to work. Circulate and provide help to students who are having difficulty.

5. When everyone is ready, discuss the results. Find out which was the heaviest book and which was the lightest book selected; next talk about the largest and the smallest books. Revisit the questions from the beginning of the lesson.

Extension

❖ Use a collection of containers that are similar to one another such as yogurt containers or plastic eggs. Fill the containers with varying amounts of sand or clay. Have children guess the containers' weights, put them in order from lightest to heaviest, and then confirm their predictions using a scale.

Objects from Nature

Overview

Children use a collection of small objects from nature and focus on their relative size and weight. Students encounter the idea that larger does not necessarily mean heavier.

Materials

❖ collection of half a dozen small natural objects from your local environment such as a stone, an acorn, a feather, a large leaf, a flower, and a pinecone
❖ box or paper bag large enough to hold the collection of small objects
❖ chart paper, 2 sheets
❖ optional: children's books that can help define the word *nature* such as *Counting on the Woods*, by George Ella Lyon (1998)
❖ optional: balance scale

Vocabulary: alike, bigger, different, heavier, larger, lighter, longer, same, shorter, size, smaller, weight

Instructions

1. Before class, place the objects you have collected in the paper bag or box.

2. To begin the lesson, invite the children to sit close enough to see each object as you reveal it. Before taking the objects from the container, ask the children to make some predictions about what you might have collected. Discuss their guesses and focus on ideas relating to size. For instance, a child might guess that you have food in the bag; another student may speculate that you have school supplies. Continue to probe their ideas and responses in order to highlight the fact that their guesses must involve objects that are small enough to fit in the container.

3. Mention the fact that you were looking for particular kinds of objects when you decided what to put in your container. Encourage the children to guess your rule and then reveal that your plan was to select objects from nature. Generate some ideas about what could *not* be in the container. Have the children identify some

objects that would be too large to fit. Ask the children to consider the weight of your collection. Ask: "What might be too heavy to fit in the box?" Pass the box or bag around so that students can heft the weight.

4. Give some advance clues about the objects that you've gathered before you reveal what you've collected. For example, you might tell the children: "None of the things that I've collected are exactly alike. Two of the items are smooth and one is bumpy. One of the things is long and another short. I found most of these things when I went on a walk near my house." Ask the children if they would like to make some new predictions.

5. Randomly reveal the objects and place them in a row so that the class can see the entire collection. Give the children a chance to inspect the objects and encourage them to describe the ways that they are alike or different.

6. To record the children's observations, write *Size* on a large piece of chart paper. Encourage the children to examine the objects carefully and to place them in order from the largest to the smallest. Ask them to explain the reason for each placement they make. When there is agreement, list the objects from *largest* to *smallest* on the chart paper. Ask the class how to explain or prove that one object is bigger than another, especially if the objects seem close in size.

7. After the size comparisons have been made and recorded, write *Weight* on another piece of chart paper and ask the children what that word means. Discuss the attribute of weight and identify tools that measure weight. Take the time to have the children relate experiences that they've had with weight, for example, at the doctor's office or in the grocery store. Pass the objects around and ask the class how to place the objects from the heaviest to the lightest. Ask if the order will be the same or different from the way they ordered the objects by size. When children are in agreement, place the objects in a line as they suggested. Ask the children how they might prove that their order is correct.

8. Share the children's book about nature. Then, have the children bring in their own items from nature so that the class can create more collections. Generate ideas for things that the children might bring to school. (You may wish to expand the types of objects beyond the original *nature* classification. Small toys would be one example.) Have the class help you compose a parent letter to explain the request and simultaneously articulate your current math focus.

9. Once the contributions begin to appear, create new collections in bags or boxes by placing six to ten objects that vary in size and weight in each container. Have students work with partners or in groups of three to *first* order the objects by size and record their findings and *then* reorganize them according to weight and record the results. Since each container will be different, students can repeat this process with more than one set of objects.

10. Ask the class if a person can tell just by looking at an object how much it weighs or whether it will be heavier or lighter than another object. Ask the children to share examples from the collection bags. Revisit this topic throughout the year.

Extension

◈ Suggest to parents that they take their children to the grocery store and have them help weigh fruits and vegetables. Have students report back to the class about the experience.

 ## Weighted Relays

Overview

Children get a chance to expend some energy as they decide which weight they would prefer to carry during a relay race—a 1-gallon container filled with water or a 1-liter container filled with water.

Materials

◈ photos, magazine pictures, and/or picture books showing people from around the world carrying water, at least 5
◈ 1-liter containers mostly filled with water, 2
◈ 1-gallon containers mostly filled with water, 2
◈ clocks or stopwatches, 2
◈ crayons, 3 to 5 per student

Vocabulary: almost, full, gallon, heavy, less, light, liter, more

Instructions

1. Begin the lesson by discussing the importance of water in our daily lives. Use the Internet, picture books, magazine pictures, or photos to help students understand that plumbing is not always available to people around the world and individuals often need to carry water from a lake or a well to their homes so that their families will have the water that they need.

2. Show the children the larger of the two containers, the *gallon* container. Explain that this would be a good container to use if your family needed water to drink, cook, and wash. Ask if anyone has seen a milk container this size. Next show the *liter* bottle and ask if anyone has seen this size when his or her family bought beverages. Tell the children that these are the two sizes that they will be comparing today.

3. Teach the children the following relay game, which can be played inside or outside. (If the game is to be played inside, take care to leave plenty of room at the top of the containers to avoid spills or use containers that can be sealed well with a lid.)

Begin by having the students divide themselves into four equal groups. There will be two teams in two sets of parallel lines opposite each other.

Team AAAAAAA   AAAAAAA
Team B B B B B B B   B B B B B B B

Give each team a 1-gallon container of water and a 1-liter container of water. Tell the class that each team will run two races. The first race will be run with the 1-gallon container. Explain that each team member is to run with the container, hand it off to a member on the opposite side of the room, and go to the back of the line, until everyone has had a turn. Instruct each team to note the time it takes to complete the race using a stopwatch or clock.

Players repeat this process using the 1-liter container, again keeping track of the time. Winning is not a focus of this particular relay. Completing the relay is the main goal.

4. When teams have finished both races, ask them to consider the following questions: Did it take longer to carry the gallon container than the liter container? Was it more difficult? Why or why not? If your goal is to transport as much water as possible, would you rather use the lighter container or the heavier one? Why? Which way would you rather fill a bathtub with water, by carrying 1-gallon containers or 1-liter containers? Why?

5. Prominently post the words *gallon, liter, weight, heavy,* and *light.* Ask the children to write and draw pictures about their experience and explain whether they would prefer to carry the lighter or the heavier amount.

6. As a class, discuss things that sometimes need to be carried considerable distances. Ask: "Why do things seem heavier over time and what are some things that people do to help heavy loads seem lighter?" Examples include a cart, wagon, or wheelbarrow.

Extensions

❧ Have the students make decisions about what kind of container they would choose if they needed to carry gallons of water to a school garden.

❧ Have children investigate how people carry water to their homes, where they get the water from, and how far they carry it.

 **Mobiles**

Overview

Making mobiles provides children with opportunities to see how weight and balance relate to each other. In this lesson, children create unique mobiles using materials such as yarn, old jewelry, hangers, and twigs.

Materials

◈ sticks, poster paper strips, and hangers, each about a foot long, enough for students to have a choice, 1 per student

◈ string, about 10–12 inches long, 1 piece per student

◈ yarn, precut to lengths of 8–10 inches, at least 3 pieces per student

◈ objects for hanging such as pinecones, old jewelry, old keys, nuts, bolts, feathers, foam shapes, and other inexpensive craft items, 3 to 6 per student

◈ camera

Note: If you know in advance that you would like to use a particular type of object, send a letter home and ask for contributions.

Vocabulary: balance, even, heavier, lighter, less, mobile, more, weight

Instructions

1. Before the lesson, make a partially completed mobile with one object hanging from the center. Set out the materials (sticks, paper strips, etc.) the children will choose from. Place the hanging objects in various locations throughout the room.

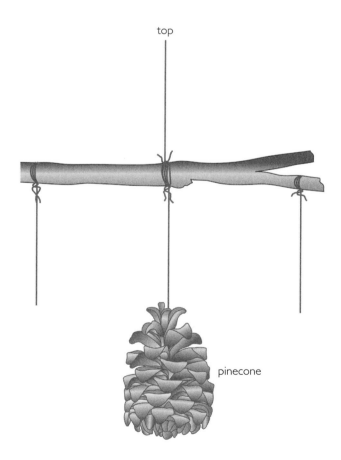

top

pinecone

2. To begin the lesson, ask the children what a mobile is. Mention crib mobiles if no one does. Show your partially completed mobile to the class. Ask the class to predict what would happen if you were to move the object from the middle to one side or the other. If someone suggests that the mobile will go down on the side with the weight, ask the student to explain further. Demonstrate what the children suggest.

3. Tell the class that everyone will have a chance to make a mobile and do some experimenting with weight. Show the materials that are available. Let the children know how many objects they should put on their mobiles. Set an exact number limit such as three, or set a range, say, from three to five.

4. Discuss tying knots. Explain that the knots they will use are *double knots*. Explain that the first step is like tying a shoe, and the second step is to repeat the process. Demonstrate as you explain. Suggest to the children that they place an object on a table or desk to tie the knot more easily. Mention that it often helps to have one person hold the object while the other person does the tying. Depending upon the age of your students, it may be helpful to invite a buddy class or volunteers to help with the knot tying.

5. Select some of the materials that you have collected and demonstrate how they can be used to create a mobile. Discuss positioning the yarn in various locations. Slide the yarn from side to side so that the weight distribution shifts. Discuss what happens, and then ask students if they think that they can look at a mobile and decide what needs to be done to make it balance.

6. Invite students to select their materials. Encourage students to assist one another as they assemble their mobiles.

7. When everyone is ready, discuss what the children made. For instance, ask the children which item on their mobile is the heaviest and how they know. Ask which item is the lightest and how they know.

8. Hang the mobiles in the room for a period of time so that students can enjoy the variations among them and further observe the relationship between weight and balance. Create a digital or paper photo record of the mobiles.

Extension

❖ Have students make straw-and-paper-clip mobile scales by doing the following:
1. Pass a straw through the widest end of a paper clip and position the clip in the center of the straw.
2. Pass a piece of yarn through the straw.
3. Tie each end of the yarn to a paper clip.
4. Pull out the ends of the dangling paper clips to form hooks.

Have students experiment with the scales by hanging a variety of objects on the hooks.

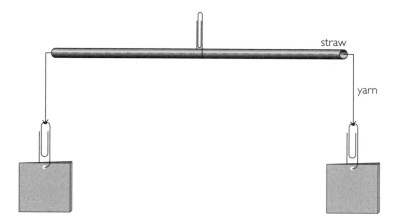

 ## Hey, What's in This Backpack, Anyway?

Overview

In this lesson, students think about the idea of reasonable weight through a silly story starter. Children are asked to estimate weight using the familiar context of filling a backpack.

Materials

- ❧ chart paper, 2–3 sheets
- ❧ 9-by-12-inch construction paper, 2 sheets
- ❧ pencils and crayons, several per student
- ❧ optional: scale

Vocabulary: carry, heavier, heaviest, heavy, lift, light, lighter, lightest, weight

Instructions

1. Before class, print the following story starter on chart paper large enough for everyone to see it: *One morning Everett P. Little had eaten a good breakfast, brushed his teeth, combed his hair, and counted out his lunch money, and he was all set to go to school. He tried to pick up his backpack and he fell right over on the floor. He said, "Hey, what's in this backpack, anyway?!"*

2. Introduce the lesson by reading the story starter. Have the children guess what Everett P. Little saw when he opened up his backpack. Explain that he repacked his backpack with exactly what he would need for the day and it was much lighter. Then, off he went to school.

3. Generate some ideas about what made the backpack so heavy and record them on the board. Remind the children that Everett P. Little repacked his backpack with lighter items. Explain that they are going to make a class book about backpacks.

Tell the children that on one side of their page they will show several things that are too heavy to carry in a backpack, and on the other side of the page they will draw several things that are light enough to carry in a backpack.

4. Make a title page, and/or use the construction paper to make book covers. Include the story starter to remind the children of the context for the lesson.

5. Give each student a sheet of 8½-by-11-inch paper and several pencils and crayons. Give them time to create their drawings.

6. Assemble the students' pages into a book. Conclude the lesson by reading the class book together.

7. If appropriate, use a scale to weigh some of the students backpacks.

Extension
◈ As a class, have students create a physical collection of both heavy objects and light objects that could fit in a backpack.

It's a Matter of Perspective

Overview
In this lesson students consider the idea that what is heavy to one person or creature may be light to another. From insects to elephants, children describe and discuss relative feats of strength. They then make a class book that reflects what they learned.

Materials
◈ images of humans at different stages of development lifting and carrying various weights and indicating a range of strength, such as

a baby carrying a toy

a child carrying a backpack

a parent carrying a child

an athlete lifting weights

an elderly person carrying groceries

(Sources for these pictures include AARP and parenting and fitness magazines.)

◈ magazine pictures, books, or Internet images that show ants, birds, horses, elephants, and other animals carrying loads
◈ chart paper, 2 or 3 sheets

Vocabulary: bigger, carry, heavier, heaviest, heavy, lift, light, lighter, lightest, older, strong, stronger, strongest, younger

Instructions

1. Meet with the children as a group and share some of your pictures of people lifting or carrying different amounts of weight. Ask the students to close their eyes and try to think back to when they were younger. Tell them to try to remember something that used to seem heavy to them and is now pretty easy to lift or carry. Inquire if anyone has a younger sister or brother who sometimes needs assistance with lifting and carrying or an older sibling who is noticeably stronger because he or she is bigger.

2. Discuss the fact that parents need to be strong enough to lift and carry babies and small children. But as the children grow up and become adults, the parents can't carry them around anymore. Give an example, such as that grandparents don't lift and carry moms and dads.

3. Using the pictures of people at various stages of development, have children speculate about other kinds of objects that the individuals would be able to lift and carry.

4. Next, show some pictures of load-carrying animals and discuss the fact that sometimes even tiny creatures can carry loads that are almost as big as they are, such as ants. Emphasize that something can be extremely heavy for one creature and very light for another.

5. On the chart paper, begin a class list with two columns, one listing animals and the other listing the items they can lift and carry. For example:

Lifters and Carriers	The Loads They Lift and Carry
ants	crumbs
spiders	insects
kangaroos	baby kangaroos (joeys)

6. Show the children the following sentences with blanks that can be filled in by using ideas from the chart. Generate some examples together.

   A _____ is heavy for a _____. A _____ is light for a _____.

   A *bug* is heavy for a *spider*. A *child* is light for a *horse*.

   A *tree* is heavy for an *elephant*. A *fish* is light for a *bear*.

7. Create a class book about lifting and carrying. Use the sentence starters from instruction 6 or have each child think of something that he or she can remember being too heavy to lift in the past that is now easy and something that he or she looks forward to being able to lift in the future.

Extension

◈ Create a class collage of lifting and carrying circumstances in the real world.

Who Sank the Boat?

Overview

Pamela Allen's rhyming story *Who Sank the Boat?* about a friendly boat ride that became a bit too crowded provides an opportunity for children to explore the question "At what point does a container become heavy enough to sink?" Students fill floating muffin cups with small objects, keeping track of how many cause the cups to sink. They then share their findings both orally and in writing.

Materials

- *Who Sank the Boat?* by Pamela Allen (1983)
- aluminum muffin cups, regular size, 1 per student
- grapes, marbles, teddy bear counters, or other small objects, a variety, about 12 per student
- small zip-top bags, 1 per student
- dishpans, 1 for each pair of students; or spreadable margarine containers, 1 per student
- water, enough to partially fill the dishpans or margarine containers

Vocabulary: fewer, float, heavy, less, light, more, same, sink, weight

Instructions

1. Prior to the lesson, prepare the materials. Into each bag, place twelve of one type of counter (use a variety of counters so that different children have different experiences). Set the bags on a table so children can choose which one they want to work with. Fill the margarine tubs or dishpans about half full with water and place them at the students' desks. Place out one dishpan per pair of students or one margarine tub per student. Also place out one muffin tin for each student.

2. Read the story *Who Sank the Boat?* and discuss the question "Could you tell who sank the boat?" Ask the children what made the boat sink and discuss the reasoning behind their opinions. Record key words from the student discussion either on the board or on word cards. Be sure to include the word *weight*. Ask the children if they have ever watched anything sink in the water. Discuss specifics about things, such as coins, toy cars, or marbles, that are heavy enough to sink in the water.

3. Show the children one of the containers of water that will be used during the class activity, either a margarine tub or a dishpan. Hold up a muffin cup and ask the students if they think that the muffin cup will sink or float. Have partners discuss their predictions. Teach the children to signal with a flat palm if they predict that the muffin cup will float or a diving motion if they predict that the cup will sink. Tell

the children that on the count of three, you want them to signal a prediction. After they have made their predictions, place the muffin cup in the water.

4. Now, tell the students that they are going to do an experiment to find out how much weight a cup can hold before it sinks. Show the students the materials they will be working with. Explain that they will add objects of their choice, one at a time, to the cup, making it heavier, like the animals in the story made the boat heavier. Make sure that the class understands that it will be important that each object is added gently. Discuss the importance of being responsible with the materials they will use. Explain the procedures for passing out and cleaning up the materials. Remind them to keep count of the number of objects that cause the cup to sink.

How many grapes will it
take to sink the muffin tin?

5. Explain that after they do the experiment, they will write and draw pictures about it, so that anyone coming into their classroom will have a clear idea of what happened during the experiment.

6. Write the following words on the board so that children can use them as needed during their recording time: *weight, sink, float, water, muffin cup,* and *grapes, marbles,* or whatever object is used to add the weight.

7. Allow children to choose their bags of counters and get to work. Circulate as students work, providing assistance when necessary.

8. Have students share their results and recordings with a partner before handing them in.

9. When everyone is ready, lead a class discussion. Begin with several empty muffin cups, filling them as students share their various results. For example, one student may have used grapes and another may have used marbles. Fill the cups with the materials that students describe. Ask questions like these:

   • Were fewer marbles consistently required to sink the cups than grapes?
   • Did all students who used the same materials get the same results?
   • What are possible reasons for differences in the results?

   Encourage students to continue to explore these questions informally at home.

Extension

❖ Repeat the experiment using a larger container than a muffin cup, for example, a microwave dinner container.

Pockets, Pockets

Overview

In this lesson children imagine that they are taking a very long walk and along the way are filling the pockets on their clothing with goodies such as coins, feathers, and rocks. Individually, they choose what to put in their pockets, keeping in mind that the longer they walk, the heavier the items will seem.

Material

❖ none

Vocabulary: big, heavier, heaviest, heavy, imaginary, light, lighter, lightest, long walk, small

Instructions

1. Begin the lesson by showing an item that you have in your pocket that is really special to you. Ask the children if they have ever carried something in a pocket that they liked *very* much. Explain that during this lesson each person is going to imagine having eight (this number can be modified according to your group) pockets on his or her clothes.

2. Continue to explain that not only will they imagine having eight pockets, but they will also imagine taking a trip to an imaginary place. Tell the children that they each can choose a place that they really know and like a lot or a place that they have never been to but would like to visit.

3. Explain more about the task. Tell the children, "One of the wonderful things about this imaginary walk is that it is just fine to fill your pockets with anything you want. The problem is that this will be a very, very *long* walk, and we all know that things seem quite heavy when you carry them for a long time. So during this walk you will need to carefully choose what to put in your pockets so that you won't get too tired."

4. Talk about what they might see as they walk. Mention to the children that along the way they could find coins, feathers, leaves, stones, nuts, pinecones, bugs, and shells. Write these ideas on the board. Ask: "What are some other things to add to our list?"

5. Now tell the children to close their eyes and go on their imaginary trips, picturing in their minds what they see, what they put in their pockets, and what they leave alone. When they are done, instruct them to draw pictures and/or write about their trips, including the things that they imagined putting in their pockets. Tell them to indicate which items are the heaviest, which ones are the lightest, which ones are the biggest, which ones are the smallest, and which one is their favorite.

6. When everyone is ready, lead a class discussion. Have children share where they went and the items they chose. Ask questions such as these:
   • Would the size of the pocket make a difference in your choice?
   • Would the biggest objects always be the heaviest objects? Can you think of examples?
   • Would it matter where the pockets were located on your clothes?
   • Would you want to fill all of the pockets?
   • Would you want one and only one object in every pocket?
   • How many items would you have if you put two things in every pocket?

Extensions
◈ Have students pair up and use balance scales to compare eight real things that could fit in pockets and order them by weight.
◈ Create a class collage of lifting and carrying circumstances in the real world.

Temperature

Introduction

No matter where we live, temperature affects our lives in fundamental ways. Children who live in areas that experience extreme temperatures develop a heightened aware-ness of temperature trends and language. Although thermometers are not always included in classroom math materials, they are readily available and quite inexpensive. It's best to use actual thermometers because temperature is such an abstract topic.

The five lessons that are included in this chapter focus attention on the language of contrasting temperatures, the use of recreational activities to adjust body temperature, thermometers as tools, and comparisons of weather temperatures from one location to another.

Hot and Cold

Overview

In this lesson, students identify things that are hot and things that are cold. They then put their ideas on paper, creating a class book of hot and cold items.

Materials
- paper, divided down the middle, labeled *hot* on one side and *cold* on the other, 1 sheet per child
- pencils and crayons, a large supply for the class to share

Vocabulary: cold, cool, dangerous, freezer, freezing, hot, refrigerator, thermostat, warm

Instructions

1. Begin the lesson by asking the children to think back to when they were very little. Ask them try to remember the first things their parents taught them about

hot and cold. (It could be that some students are currently experiencing these early lessons with younger siblings.) Have them describe what they remember. Most children will likely remember that they were warned to stay away from stoves, ovens, curling irons, and other hot appliances.

2. Next, ask them if they can remember a cool or cold place in their home. Remind the children of the sensation of opening the door of a refrigerator and feeling the cool air on their faces. Explain that the ideas of hot and cold are math ideas because they can be described with numbers. Ask the children if they have ever noticed the thermostats or dials with numbers in their refrigerators or on their ovens or the thermostats in their homes. Mention that adults need to pay attention to how hot or how cold things get and they use those numbers to keep track of and control the temperature.

3. Tell the students that each of them will make a page for a class book about things that are hot and things that are cold. Distribute the prepared sheets, pointing out the two columns and their labels. Tell students to write about or draw things that are hot in the appropriate column, and in the other column to write about or draw things that are cold. Ask children to share some thoughts about things that are hot and things that are cold with classmates who are sitting near them before they begin to record. As students finish, display the pages in the classroom before compiling them into a class book. The cover or title page of the book could include pictures or drawings of thermostats to reinforce the numerical connection.

4. Read the class book together and compare the children's responses. Look for common themes and ideas.

Extensions
◈ Have children create pages of things that are *warm* and things that are *cool* and compile the pages into a class book.
◈ Connect symbolic temperatures with hot and cold by discussing typical household temperature devices such as thermostats.

 ## Temperatures of Food

Overview
In this lesson students reflect on grocery shopping and cooking experiences to think about temperatures of food. They identify what foods must be kept hot and what must be kept cold and learn the reasons it is important to store food at its proper temperature.

Materials

◈ grocery store food advertisements, 4 to 6

◈ chart paper, 1 or 2 sheets

Vocabulary: fresh, frozen, refrigerated

Instructions

1. Show the children grocery store food advertisements and ask students to raise their hands if they ever help with grocery shopping.

2. Tell the class that grocery store owners are careful to organize their goods in particular ways. Ask: "Have you noticed that you can anticipate exactly where to find things in your grocery store?" Record students' observations on chart paper as they describe the sorting and classifying systems in their grocery stores.

3. Explain that a long time ago, before there was electricity for refrigerators, people used to keep food cold with huge chunks of ice. Tell students that no matter how we keep food cold, it is very important for our health that cold and hot foods are kept at the correct temperatures; otherwise, they can make us sick.

4. Ask the children to think about what happens to the food once it gets home from the grocery store. Distribute blank 8½-by-11-inch paper. Have each child either (1) draw a diagram of a kitchen to show where cold things are stored and hot things prepared or (2) draw pictures or make a list of food items that need to be kept cold and those that are prepared hot.

5. Have a class sharing session about the student work that was created during the lesson. Discuss ways that lunches are prepared for school, and use milk as an example of a food that must be refrigerated for health reasons.

Extension

◈ Have each child draw a map of his or her grocery store.

Fun with Water

Overview

In this lesson, children develop awareness about the ways people have fun with water, how to keep cool, and how to warm up. Children learn benchmark temperatures for judging when temperatures are hot and when they are cold.

Materials

❖ large calendar or magazine pictures of people enjoying water fun and sports such as swimming, playing at water parks, skiing, ice-skating, and sledding, 6 to 8

❖ large paper thermometer (see Blackline Masters)

❖ crayons, several for each child

Vocabulary: cold, cool off, extreme, Fahrenheit, hot, temperature, warm up, 0°, 32°, 90°

Instructions

1. Before the lesson, prepare a large paper thermometer marked at 32° Fahrenheit and 90° Fahrenheit.

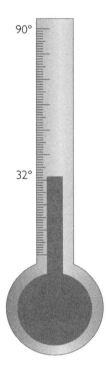

2. Invite the children to sit near you, and ask if anyone can remember being extremely hot or cold. Discuss what they did to get more comfortable. Ask the class if it is more likely in your area of the country to get extremely hot or to get extremely cold. If you have both kinds of temperatures, discuss which extreme happens more often.

3. Show the children how to write 90° and 32° and find their location on the paper thermometer. Explain that 90 degrees is uncomfortably hot for many people. Further explain that the opposite of hot is cold and that water freezes at 32 degrees.

4. Tell the class that this lesson will be about ways that water can help people adjust their body temperatures. Explain, for example, that water parks help people cool off on hot days, and that on cold days, people can use frozen water to get exercise by going ice-skating, skiing, or sledding and then enjoy having hot chocolate to warm up.

5. Point out that there are many ways to just have fun with water, like walking in puddles, taking a walk with an umbrella, making a snow fort, playing in the sprinkler, or playing in a warm tub. Share the prepared pictures that show people enjoying water. Ask each child to draw a picture to show himself or herself enjoying a favorite water, ice, or snow pastime.

6. During a whole-class discussion after children have completed their drawings, make a list of the different water recreations that have been recorded. Have the class decide whether the activities were done in the summer to *cool off* or in the winter to *warm up*. Look at the number of pictures that show cooling-off activities and the amount that show warming-up activities and compare the amounts.

Extension
◈ Have the children survey people in the school to see if most people would rather use water recreation to cool off on hot days or warm up on cold days.

 ## Thermometers as Tools

Overview
Young children have very real contextual experience with temperatures in their local environments. In this lesson, students use local temperatures to think about temperatures as vertical number lines.

Materials
◈ large outdoor vertical thermometers, at least 1
◈ paper thermometers 4 per student (see Blackline Masters)
◈ newspaper or Internet weather report of the current temperature

Vocabulary: above zero, below zero, cold, counting numbers (by tens), degree, Fahrenheit, hot, temperature, thermometer, zero, °

Instructions

1. Begin the lesson with a talk about *the weather*. Discuss both the most pleasant and the most challenging weather in your area. Weather is relevant to children and adults alike, since it affects how we dress, our transportation, and, perhaps most importantly for the children, recess.

2. Show the class the large outdoor thermometer. Explain that a thermometer is designed like a number line that goes up and down instead of straight across or left to right. Place a piece of paper over the thermometer at 0, and count the numbers by tens going up to 100. Emphasize that each of the smaller lines represents individual counting numbers and increase by one.

3. Explain that the numbers on the thermometer indicate how hot or cold it is outside and that the higher the number, the hotter the temperature is. Tell the class the following:
   • Some places in the world get very hot and the numbers get higher.
   • Others get very cold and the numbers get lower.
   • Some places get so cold that the measurement is less than zero, which is why there are numbers below the 0.

   Discuss the place that you live and the temperatures that you commonly experience.

4. Show the children a copy of the paper thermometer. Explain that on a real thermometer there is a glass tube with red liquid inside that rises as the temperature gets hotter. Find a good location to place the outside thermometer so the class can keep track of the temperature on a daily basis. If possible, position several outdoor thermometers in various locations around the school, for instance, in the shade and in the sun, so that they can be compared.

5. Ask the students what they expect the thermometer to read at this moment and why. Ask what they expect for the next month and why. Explain that during the next month, each person in the class will record the temperature once a week. Have students use the paper thermometers as their recording sheets. The thermometer at school can be used as a source as well as published resources. Show the class some additional sources for weather information, such as television, newspapers, and the Internet.

6. After each recording of the temperature, ask the children to describe the weather for that day in their own words. Discuss the role that the temperature plays in the weather. Ask: "Does temperature alone completely describe the weather? How important is temperature? If the temperature is very hot or very cold, how much does that matter to us?" Post a completed, dated paper thermometer along with the class description of the weather for that day. Compare and discuss the recordings over time.

Extensions
◈ Have the class keep track of the temperature over an extended period of time such as once a week all year long.

◈ See how many different kinds of thermometers the class can identify and how each is used. Some examples are thermostats, oven thermometers, thermometers to check to see if someone has a fever, meat thermometers, candy thermometers, dial thermometers, and digital thermometers.

 ## How's the Weather?

Overview
In this lesson students study a map of the United States to select two or three places that are of particular interest to them. Over time they systematically keep track of the weather in those places and make temperature comparisons with their own location.

Materials
◈ large classroom map of the United States
◈ pointer or yardstick
◈ dot stickers, 1 per child
◈ Internet resources or newspapers from the locations under study

Vocabulary: east, names of locations, north, south, west

Instructions

1. Begin the lesson by displaying a large classroom map of the United States. Ask the children to name places that they have traveled to or places where they have relatives. Indicate with a pointer or yardstick each location on the map that the children mention and then place a dot sticker on those locations. As children share, you will get a sense of their concepts of space: Some children may spend a good deal of time and conversation determining where they live in relation to the rest of the country; others may have little understanding of geographical relationships. This quick and easy activity helps children develop map skills, and it also helps them get to know each other.

2. Point out a few locations that appear to have very different environments than your own, and suggest to the class that it would be interesting to know what the weather is like in these places. Have the students narrow the list to the two or three places that they are most interested in.

3. Now have students begin to collect and record weather data for the places that the class has selected as well as your own area. Help them use the Internet or newspapers to obtain the information. Agree to collect data about high temperatures and

use the recording method that is the best match with your usual classroom routines. For example, if you typically discuss weather events during calendar time, it would be logical to record the information during that routine. If your students regularly use math journals, incorporate the organization of data in the journals.

4. Ask students to compare the temperatures and discuss what they notice. Ask: "Which place is the hottest? The coldest? Does it seem like it is usually hotter or colder in that place than it is here? Why do you think so?"

5. Have students discuss their results in relation to your own environment and temperatures.

Extension

◈ Have students and parents choose a place where a relative or friend lives and keep track of the temperatures in that location. Possibly, have each student develop a pen-pal relationship with a student in that location so that they can share personal impressions of the climate.

Blackline Masters

Compared with My Yarn

Three Bears

Three Bowls

Three Chairs

Three Beds

Name Trains

Around the Shape: Trapezoid

Around the Shape: Rectangle

Around the Shape: Triangle

Around the Shape: Square

Growing Things

Bird Drawings 1

Bird Drawings 2

Bird Drawings 3

Inch Strip and Centimeter Strip

Foot Race

Pictures of George

More Pictures of George

Sixty-Second/Sixty-Minute Clock Display

Blank Clock Faces

Clock Puzzle

10-by-10 Grid

Yarn Loops

Box Bases

Is It Half?

Compared with Your Hand

The Right Fit

What Unit Did You Use?

Origami Cup Directions

Half-Inch Grid Paper

Thermometer

Compared with My Yarn

Longer

Shorter

Three Bears

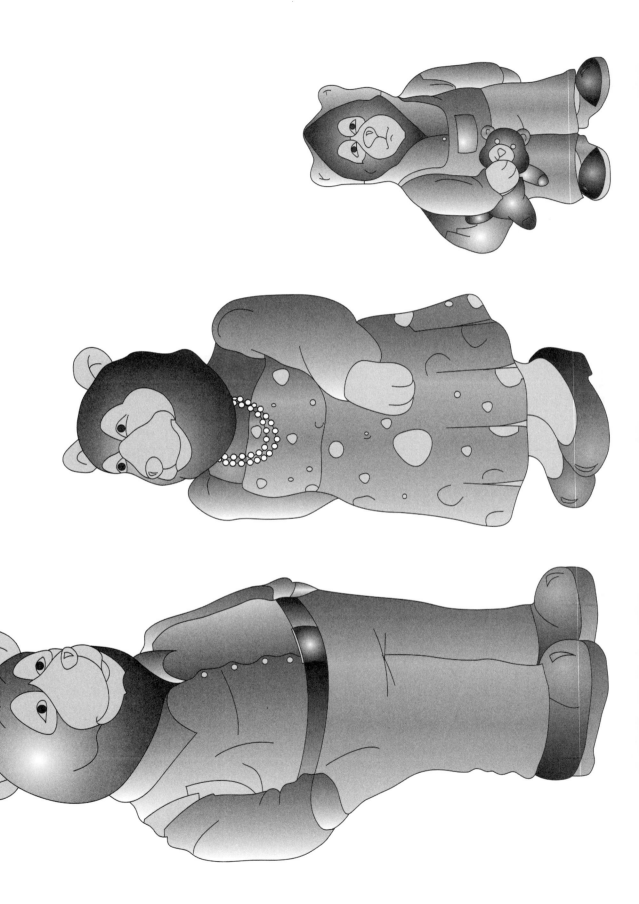

Three Bowls

Three Chairs

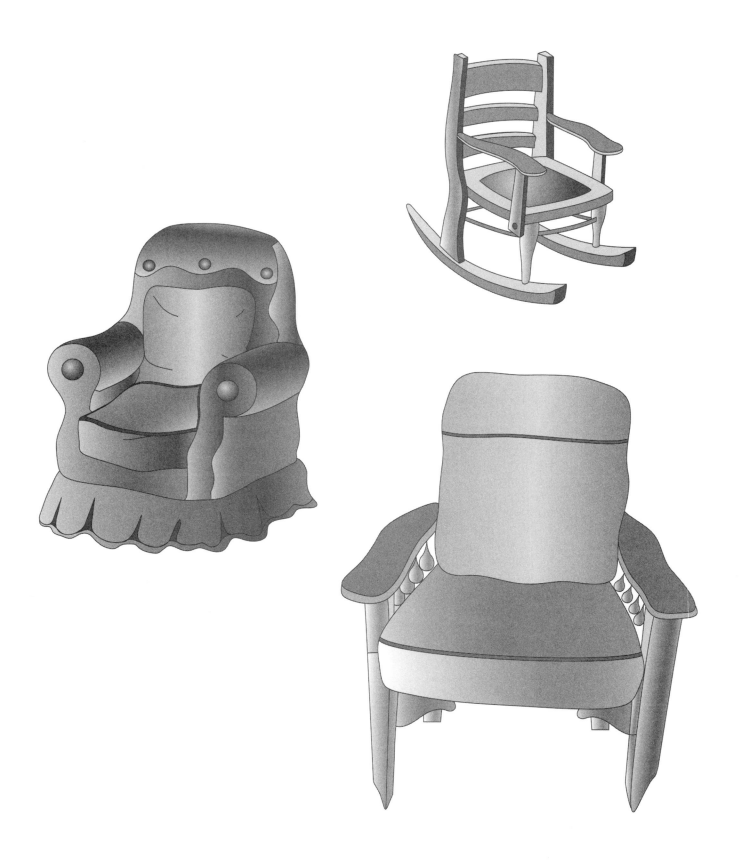

Three Beds

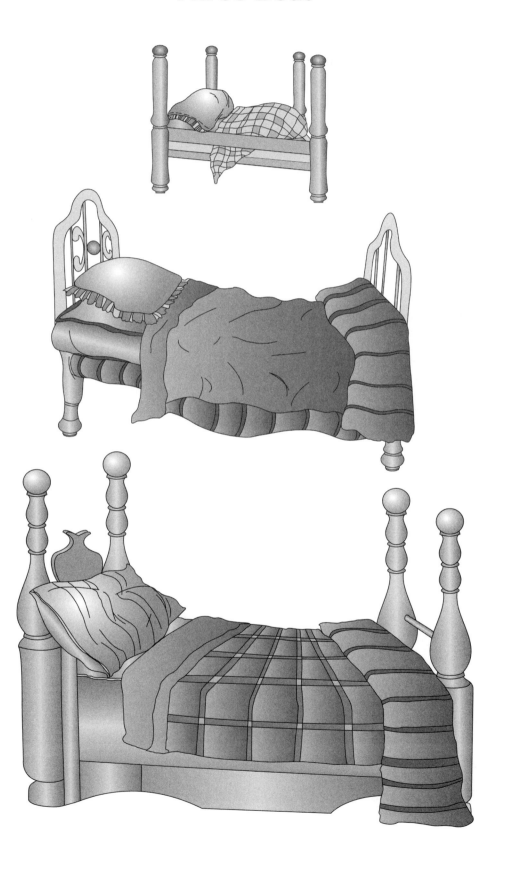

Name Trains

Partner 1	
Partner 2	

The name _____ is **shorter**.

The name _____ is **longer**.

The name _____ is _____ cube(s) longer than _____.

Or

Both _____ and _____ are the **same length**.

Around the Shape: Trapezoid

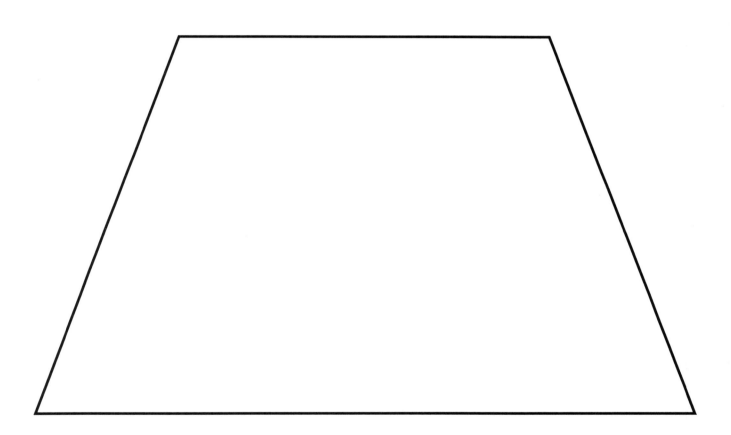

Around the Shape: Rectangle

Around the Shape: Triangle

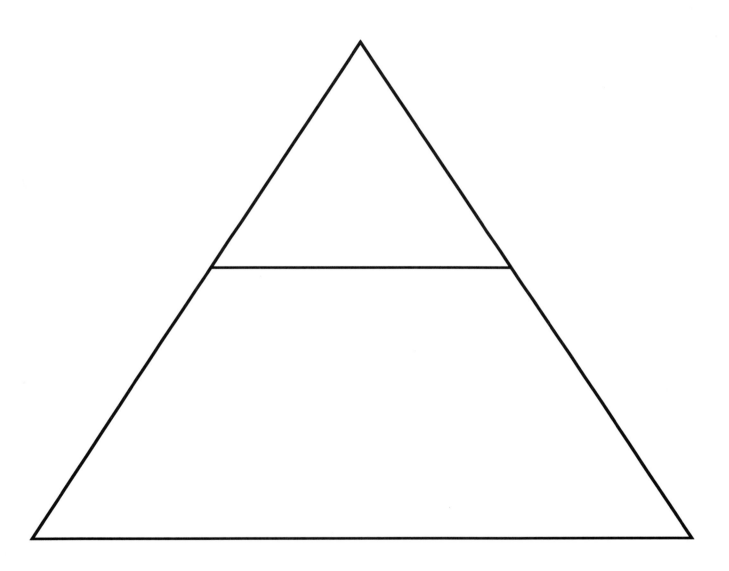

Around the Shape: Square

Growing Things

Name: _____

I am observing seed number: _____

Week 1	Week 2	Week 3
Week 4	Week 5	Week 6

Bird Drawings 1

The distance between
my points is _____ .

The distance between
my points is _____ .

From *Sizing Up Measurement: Activities for Grades K–2 Classrooms* by Vicki Bachman. © 2007 by Math Solutions Publications.

Bird Drawings 2

The distance between
my points is _____ .

The distance between
my points is _____ .

Bird Drawings 3

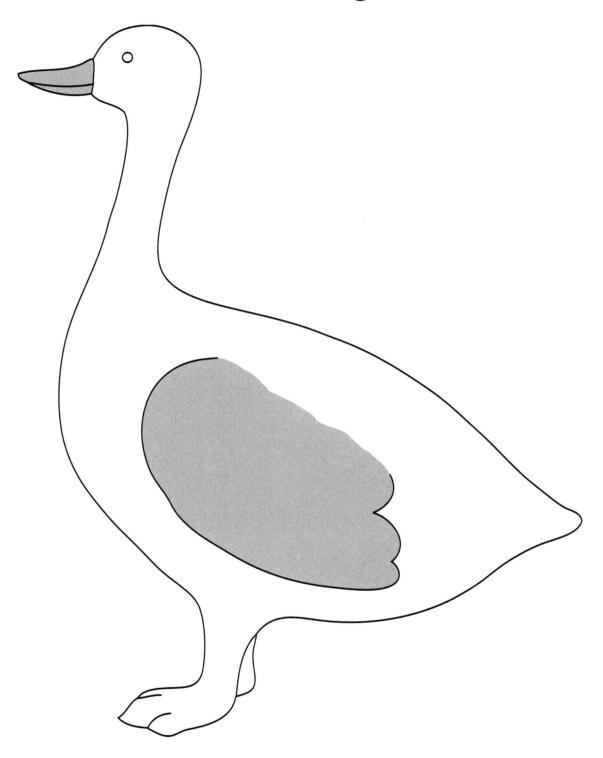

The distance between
my points is _____.

Inch Strip and Centimeter Strip

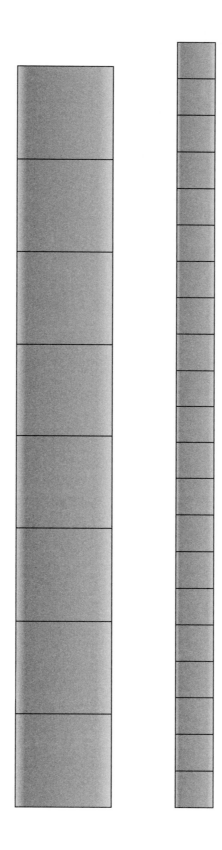

Foot Race

Game 1

I rolled: _____   _____

            _____   _____

            _____   _____

            _____   _____

            _____   _____

            _____

I had exactly 12 when I went out.   Yes or No

Game 2

I rolled: _____   _____

            _____   _____

            _____   _____

            _____   _____

            _____   _____

            _____

I had exactly 12 when I went out.   Yes or No

Game 3

I rolled: _____   _____

            _____   _____

            _____   _____

            _____   _____

            _____   _____

I had exactly 12 when I went out.   Yes or No

Pictures of George

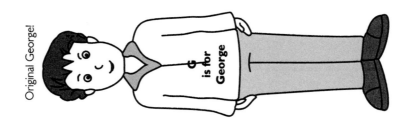

Original George!

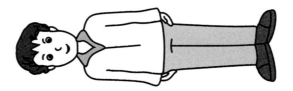

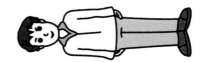

More Pictures of George

Sixty-Second/Sixty-Minute Clock Display

60 seconds = 1 minute
60 minutes = 1 hour

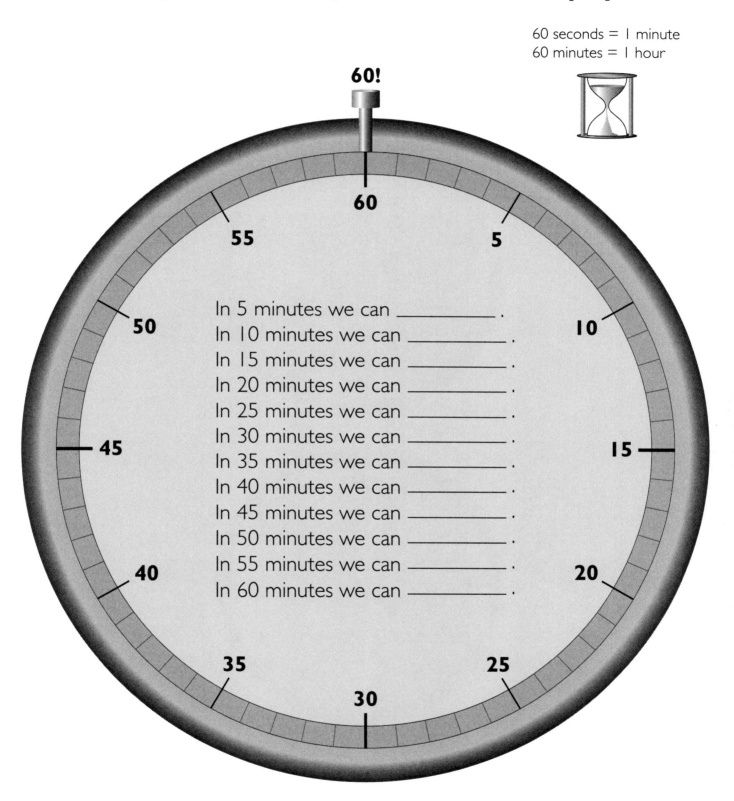

60!

60

55   5

50   10

45   15

In 5 minutes we can _____ .
In 10 minutes we can _____ .
In 15 minutes we can _____ .
In 20 minutes we can _____ .
In 25 minutes we can _____ .
In 30 minutes we can _____ .
In 35 minutes we can _____ .
In 40 minutes we can _____ .
In 45 minutes we can _____ .
In 50 minutes we can _____ .
In 55 minutes we can _____ .
In 60 minutes we can _____ .

40   20

35   25

30

Color one segment each day. Change colors when you get to a pattern-of-five number to better visualize each five-minute section.

From *Sizing Up Measurement: Activities for Grades K–2 Classrooms* by Vicki Bachman. © 2007 by Math Solutions Publications.

Blank Clock Faces

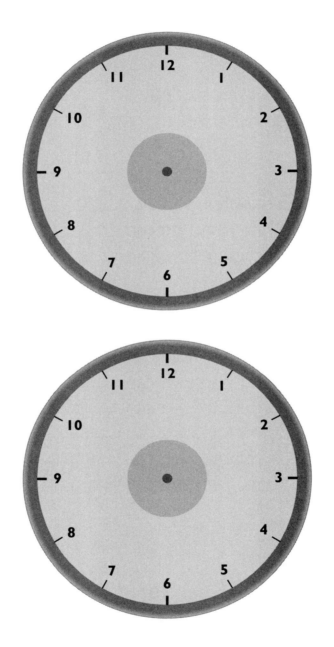

Clock Puzzle

Hour Hand

Use a brad to connect.

Cut and paste.

| 1 | 2 | 3 | 4 | 5 | 6 | 7 | 8 | 9 | 10 | 11 | 12 |

10-by-10 Grid

Yarn Loops

My yarn loop looked like this:

I counted _____.

Box Bases

We predict that _____ will fit.

We counted _____.

Show the tiles in your box.

Is It Half?

9 squares

4 squares

6 squares

___ filled in

___ blank

___ filled in

___ blank

___ filled in

___ blank

16 squares

12 squares

___ filled in

___ blank

___ filled in

___ blank

Compared with Your Hand

Show 3 things that are smaller than your hand:

1.

2.

3.

Show 3 things that are bigger than your hand:

1.

2.

3.

5th

4th

Fold Here

3rd

2nd

1st

What Unit Did You Use?

We picked container number _____.

We will use (circle one):

    I cup scoop $\frac{1}{2}$ *cup scoop*   *I tablespoon scoop*

We think it will take _____ scoops to fill our container.

It took _____ scoops.

Next we will use (circle one):

    I cup scoop $\frac{1}{2}$ *cup scoop*   *I tablespoon scoop*

We think it will take _____ scoops to fill our container.

It took _____ scoops.

_____

We picked container number _____.

We will use (circle one):

    I cup scoop $\frac{1}{2}$ *cup scoop*   *I tablespoon scoop*

We think it will take _____ scoops to fill our container.

It took _____ scoops.

Next we will use (circle one):

    I cup scoop $\frac{1}{2}$ *cup scoop*   *I tablespoon scoop*

We think it will take _____ scoops to fill our container.

It took _____ scoops.

Origami Cup Directions

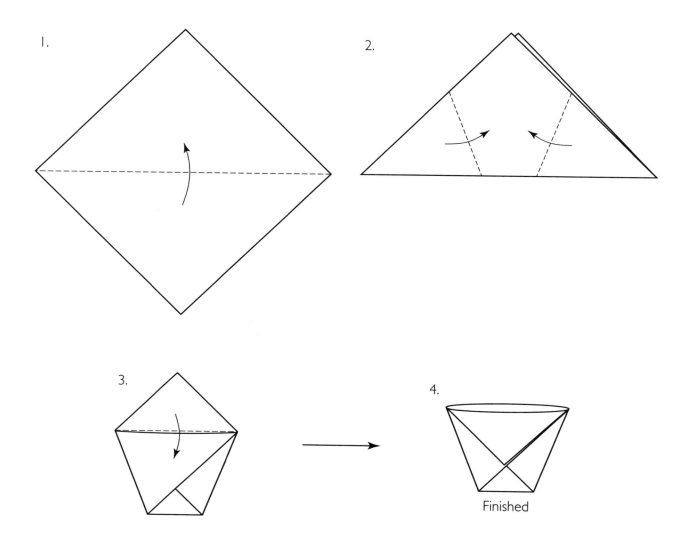

1.

2.

3.

4.

Finished

Half-Inch Grid Paper

Thermometer

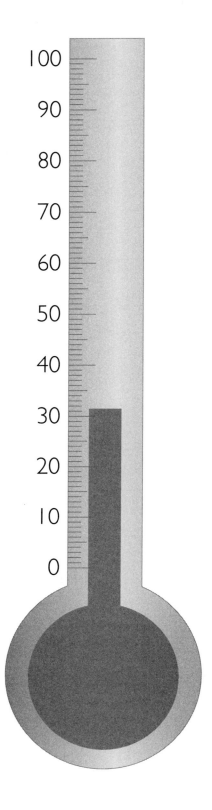

Glossary

We've included in the glossary mathematical terms, phrases, and expressions that relate to measurement and are used in the K–2 book or the 3–5 book. Whenever possible, we use the correct terminology in the context of activities, often pairing the mathematical terminology with words students commonly understand. For example, when introducing the word *polygon*, we might use the word *shape* as well. During a lesson, we highlight key vocabulary for students, sometimes by recording these words on a vocabulary word chart. When appropriate, we encourage students to use this language as they discuss their thinking with each other and as they record their ideas in writing. In this way, over time, students acquire the language of mathematics.

A.M.: ante meridiem; between midnight and noon

acute angle: an angle that measures between 0 degrees and 90 degrees; an angle having a measure that is less than a right angle

analog clock: a clock that shows the numerals 1–12, with a longer pointer to indicate the hour and a shorter pointer to indicate the minute

angle: a figure consisting of two rays with the same end point; its size is measured by the amount one ray has rotated in relation to the other

area: the measure of the amount of surface inside a closed boundary

array: a rectangular arrangement in rows and columns

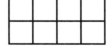

average: a typical or middle value for a set of numbers

balance scale: an instrument used to measure mass or weight; an object is placed in a weighing pan and a combination of standard weights are placed in a scale pan; standard weights are added to the scale pan until the pans are balanced

benchmark: a familiar length or object that is used as a point of reference to compare in estimation; a referent

Celsius: a scale for temperature measurement: water freezes at 0°C and boils at 100°C

centimeter: in the metric system, a unit of length equivalent to 10 millimeters or $\frac{1}{100}$ meter

circle: the set of all points in a plane that are the same distance (radius) from a point (the center of the circle)

circumference: the distance around a circle or sphere

column: a vertical arrangement of objects or numbers in an array or table

concave polygon: a polygon with at least one interior angle greater than 180 degrees

cone: a three-dimensional shape having a circular base, curved surface, and one vertex

conjecture: a reasonable guess

convex polygon: a polygon with all interior angles less than 180 degrees

cube: a three-dimensional shape with six square faces

customary units: units used in the United States for measuring length, volume, weight, and temperature; for example, inches, teaspoons, and pounds

cylinder: a three-dimensional shape with a curved surface and parallel, circular bases that are the same size

decimal: a number written in standard notation, often containing a decimal point, as in 3.45

decimeter: in the metric system, a unit of length equivalent to 10 centimeters or $\frac{1}{10}$ meter

degree: a unit of measure for temperature or angles; for angles, $\frac{1}{360}$ of a circle

diagonal: an arrangement of objects or numbers in an array or table from upper right to lower left or upper left to lower right

digital clock: clock that uses numbers to show the time in hours and minutes with a colon used to separate them, such as 3:20 A.M.

dimensions: a measure in one direction; for example, length, width, or height

distance: how far away something is; distance is measured in units of length

elapsed time: the amount of time between a beginning time and an ending time

end point: one of the points at each end of a line segment; the point at the end of a ray

equivalent: having the same value

estimate: a reasonable guess; a calculation of a close, instead of an exact, answer

Fahrenheit: a temperature scale; water freezes at 32°F and boils at 212°F

fluid ounce: in the customary system, a unit of capacity or volume; $\frac{1}{8}$ cup

foot: in the customary system, a unit of length equivalent to 12 inches or $\frac{1}{3}$ yard

gallon: in the customary system, a unit of capacity or volume containing 128 ounces

gram: a unit of mass equal to $\frac{1}{1,000}$ kilogram

heft: a hand movement used to estimate or compare weights

height: distance upward from a given point

hemisphere: half of a sphere

hexagon: a polygon with six sides

improper fraction: a fraction that names a number greater than or equal to 1; for example, $\frac{5}{4}$ or $\frac{8}{6}$

inch: in the customary system, a unit of length equal to $\frac{1}{12}$ foot

iteration: repeating the same steps or process over and over; unit iteration is the repetition of a single unit. If you are measuring the length of a desk with straws, it is easy to lay out straws across the desk and then count them. But if only one straw is available, then you must iterate (repeat) the unit (straw)

kilogram: in the metric system, a unit of mass equal to 1,000 grams

length: a measure of how long something is; length is measured in inches, centimeters, and so on

line segment: part of a line with two end points

liter: in the metric system, a unit of capacity or volume; a little less than a quart

mass: the amount of matter in an object; mass is usually measured against an object of known mass, often in grams or kilograms

mean: a typical value of a set of numbers

median: the middle data point in a set of data arranged in order of value

meter: in the metric system, a unit of length equal to 100 centimeters

metric system: a system of measurement built on the base ten numeration system; the units of measure in this system include millimeters, centimeters, meters, and kilometers for length, liters and milliliters for volume, grams and kilograms for weight, and degrees Celsius for temperature

millimeter: in the metric system, a unit of length equal to $\frac{1}{10}$ centimeter or $\frac{1}{1,000}$ meter

mode: the most frequently occurring data value in a graph

obtuse angle: an angle that measures between 90 degrees and 180 degrees

open number line: a number line with only the numbers relevant to a specific computational strategy. For example, for 36 + ___ = 60:

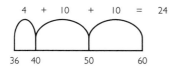

ounce: in the customary system, a unit of weight or volume; $\frac{1}{16}$ pound or $\frac{1}{8}$ cup, respectively

P.M.: post meridiem; between noon and midnight

parallelogram: a quadrilateral that has two pairs of parallel sides; opposite sides are the same length

perimeter: the distance around a two-dimensional shape

pint: in the customary system, a unit of capacity or volume equivalent to 2 cups or 16 fluid ounces

polygon: a closed two-dimensional figure made of line segments (sides) connected at their end points

pound: in the customary system, a unit of weight equivalent to 16 ounces

protractor: a device for measuring or drawing angles

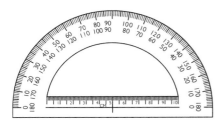

quadrilateral: a polygon with four sides

quart: in the customary system, a unit of capacity or volume equivalent to 4 cups or 32 fluid ounces

range: the difference between the least and greatest values in a distribution

ray: part of a line with one end point

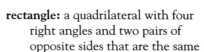

rectangle: a quadrilateral with four right angles and two pairs of opposite sides that are the same length

rectangular prism: a prism that has rectangles for all the faces

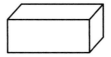

referent: a benchmark; a familiar length or object that is used as a point of reference to compare in estimation

rhombus: a parallelogram with all sides the same length

right angle: an angle that measures exactly 90 degrees

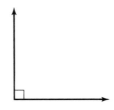

rotate: to turn around a center point

sample: a representative part of an entire set used to gather information about the whole group

scale: a way to measure length or distance with a graduated sequence of marks; an instrument for measuring weight

side: any of the line segments forming a polygon

spring scale: a type of scale used for measuring mass or weight; a spring scale determines an item's weight by identifying how far a spring stretches against a written scale

square: a rectangle with four sides that are the same length

square centimeter: in the metric system, a unit of area that is a square that has the measure of each side equal to 1 centimeter

straight angle: an angle measuring exactly 180 degrees

tablespoon: in the customary system, a unit of capacity or volume; 3 teaspoons or $\frac{1}{16}$ cup

teaspoon: in the customary system, a unit of capacity or volume; $\frac{1}{6}$ fluid ounce

thermometer: an instrument used to display temperature

three-dimensional object: an object that has length, width, and depth; objects that fill space as prisms, pyramids, and spheres

time line: a scaled line used to display a certain length of time; a time line often has events displayed in positions according to when they occurred

ton: a unit of weight; in the U.S. system, 2,000 pounds

transitivity: a mathematical property that states, "If A = B and B = C, then A = C; if A < B and B < C, then A < C; if A > B and B > C, then A > C"; in measurement, when you can't compare two objects directly, you must compare them by means of a third object, for example, a ruler

trapezoid: a quadrilateral with exactly one pair of parallel sides

triangle: a polygon with three sides

unit: a label, word, or unit of measure used with a number to show its size or context; for example, inches, quarts, centimeters, degrees

U.S. customary system: system that measures length in inches, feet, yards, and miles, for example; capacity in cups, pints, quarts, and gallons, for example; weight in ounces, pounds, and tons, for example; and temperature in degrees Fahrenheit

vertex: a point where rays of an angle or sides of a polygon meet

vertical: straight up and down

volume: the measure of how much space a three-dimensional shape fills

weight: a measure of how heavy something is; measured in units including ounces, pounds, grams, and kilograms

width: the horizontal measurement made at a right angle to the height

yard: in the customary system, a unit of length equal to 3 feet or 36 inches

References

Aber, Linda Williams. 2001. *Carrie Measures Up!* New York: Kane.

Adler, David. 1999. *How Tall, How Short, How Far Away.* New York: Holiday House.

Allen, Pamela. 1983. *Who Sank the Boat?* New York: Coward-McCann.

Axelrod, Amy. 1997. *Pigs in the Pantry: Fun with Math and Cooking.* New York: Simon and Schuster Books for Young Readers.

———. 1998. *Pigs on a Blanket: Fun with Math and Time.* New York: Aladdin.

Baker, Alan. 1999. *Little Rabbit's First Time Book.* New York: Kingfisher.

Brett, Jan. 1989. *The Mitten: A Ukrainian Folktale.* New York: Putnam.

Bunting, Eve. 1989. *The Wednesday Surprise.* New York: Clarion.

Carle, Eric. 1990. *The Tiny Seed.* Saxonville, MA: Picture Book Studio.

———. 1996. *The Grouchy Ladybug.* New York: HarperCollins.

Dooley, Norah. 1991. *Everybody Cooks Rice.* Minneapolis: Carolrhoda.

Edwards, Pamela Duncan. 1998. *Warthogs in the Kitchen: A Sloppy Counting Book.* New York: Hyperion Books for Children.

Firefly Books. 2003. *Firefly Guide to Flags Around the World.* New York: Firefly Books.

Ford, Miela. 1995. *Sunflower.* New York: Greenwillow.

Gibbons, Gail. 1979. *Clocks and How They Go.* New York: Crowell.

———. 1984. *The Seasons of Arnold's Apple Tree.* San Diego: Harcourt Brace Jovanovich.

———. 1991. *From Seed to Plant.* New York: Holiday House.

———. 1995. *The Reasons for Seasons.* New York: Holiday House.

Johnson, Neil. 1997. *A Field of Sunflowers*. New York: Scholastic.

Joyce, William. 1985. *George Shrinks*. New York: Harper and Row.

King, Carole. 2004. "Chicken Soup with Rice." *Really Rosie*. Sony. Compact disc.

Lionni, Leo. 1967. *Frederick*. New York: Pantheon.

———. 1992. *A Busy Year*. New York: Scholastic.

———. 1995. *Inch by Inch*. New York: Mulberry.

Lyon, George Ella. 1998. *Counting on the Woods: A Poem*. New York: DK.

Minarik, Else H. 1957. *Little Bear*. New York: HarperTrophy.

Morris, Ann. 1989. *Hats, Hats, Hats*. New York: Lothrop, Lee and Shepard.

Osborne, Mary P. 2001. Magic Tree House Series. New York: Random House Books for Young Readers.

Rathmann, Peggy. 1998. *10 Minutes till Bedtime*. New York: G. P. Putnam's Sons.

Russo, Marisabina. 1992. *The Line Up Book*. New York: Puffin.

Ryder, Stephanie. 1996. *Tell Time at the Farm*. London: Brimax.

Sendak, Maurice. 1962. *Chicken Soup with Rice: A Book of Months*. New York: Harper.

Slobodkina, Esphyr. 1985. *Caps for Sale: A Tale of a Peddler, Some Monkeys, and Their Monkey Business*. New York: Harper and Row.

Tompert, Ann. 1993. *Just a Little Bit*. Boston: Houghton Mifflin.

Index